A LIFE WORTH
LIVING

A LIFE BLESSED BY GOD

DR. ROBERT H. PINDER

A LIFE WORTH
LIVING

A LIFE BLESSED BY GOD

XULON PRESS

Xulon Press
2301 Lucien Way #415
Maitland, FL 32751
407.339.4217
www.xulonpress.com

Unless otherwise indicated, Scripture quotations taken from the Holy
Bible, New International Version (NIV). Copyright © 1973, 1978, 1984,
2011 by Biblica, Inc.™. Used by permission. All rights reserved.

Printed in the United States of America.

ISBN-13: 978-1-5456-7294-5

INTRODUCTION

I want this to be a testimony of God, His Grace, Mercy and Love. I want to be sure and give God the glory for what He was able to accomplish in my life. God doesn't call the qualified, He qualifies the called. His Grace is more than enough for any task. My response to His call — over 80 years a committed Christian and servant. Our devotional this morning is my daily prayer.

A Prayer, to be Humble

God, who made the world and everything in it, since He is Lord of heaven and earth, does not dwell in temples made with hands. Acts 17:24

> My Father, I desire that the attitude of John the Baptist might be my own–that Jesus would increase even as I decrease. Give me an ever larger picture of you so I might see myself with ever-increasing clarity and revel each day in your amazing grace. Keep foolish pride far from me, and give me the sense to humble myself in healthy ways that bring strength and joy to everyone around me. Remind me constantly, Lord, that you hold my life and breath and eternal future in your loving hands and that every good thing I have comes from you. Never

let me forget that although without you I can do nothing, in Christ I Can do all things. The difference is you. In Jesus' name I pray, Amen.

Also, this book is filled with names and experiences of mentors, pastors, teachers and friends who have helped to form my life and influence me for good. I regret that I waited until my 90th year to get serious about writing a book. My memory is not what it was 10 years ago. But worst of all, I have outlived all of my peers. I had a strong, active group of preacher friends in Florida but all of them have passed on. I found two great friends, but both said they had dementia and could not write anything about our relationship. I am a collector. Throughout my life I have saved everything, especially anything family or personal. I have always written a lot to my family, especially since email and texting became available. I put together some of those writings and sent them to my children. They encouraged me to write more. They surprised me with a wonderful 90th birthday celebration. They showed photos and videos of my life and God told me that I am obligated to publicly share my testimony with my extended family and beyond. He reminded me how much He had blessed me, and invested so much in my life. God showed me how many mentors and friends had helped me and supported me all along the way. I am inspired and helped by the letters from former students and friends who have written testimonies of how God has blessed and multiplied my life.

I have a stack of letters and awards 10 inches high. I set up 38 folders, representing segments of time, and put those papers piece by piece into those folders. I will do the best that I can writing on my own, and supplementing with testimonies and other materials to complete what I hope will be a good testimony of the life that God has so blessed. Writing this book has been the hardest thing that I have ever attempted. If I had known how difficult it would be, I would never have started. But now it is God's mandate for me.

The little that I have shared of my story so far, has found a warm response. I pray it will be a blessing to you.

Chapter One

TWO GREAT HONORS
IN MY 90ᵀᴴ YEAR

I taught Human Development and Family Studies at Texas Tech University for 23 years. I will share more later. I love teaching. I love the students. There are testimonies from students, faculty, and university administrators throughout this book. I had a strong Christian testimony on campus. I started a faculty Bible study. I was a faculty sponsor for five Christian student organizations on campus. I majored in Baptist student work in college, and have been active in Baptist student ministry ever since. I helped to build a new Baptist student union building at Texas A&M University, East Texas, and North Texas. I kept asking when will we build a new BSM building at Texas Tech. Finally they are building a new Baptist Student Ministry building at Texas Tech, and naming it in my honor. The new building will be named the DR. ROBERT H. PINDER STUDENT CENTER. What an honor, reaching students for Jesus for generations to come.

Also, this year at the annual convention of the Baptist General Convention of Texas, Bill Arnold, President of the Texas Baptist Missions Foundation presented me the Adventurer Award for Leadership in Missions.

As a teenager, I was running with the wrong crowd. When God brought me back to Himself and an active youth group in

1

church, He called me into the ministry with a burning conviction, EVERYBODY NEEDS THE LORD. And that has been my passion all my life. Missions and evangelism has captivated everything I have ever done, my college years, the pastorates, mission service in Argentina, teaching students, and retirement.

Bill Arnold, President of the Missions Foundation of the Baptist General Convention of Texas, announced the award and introduced Don Cramer who made the presentation. My family was present for the award dinner.

Bill Arnold's Testimony:

What a privilege it has been for me to count Bob Pinder as a friend. No matter where or how Bob served the Lord – as a pastor, missionary, professor or Baptist Student Ministry volunteer – he has been a role model and mentor to everyone whose life touched his. As a member of the Texas Missions Foundation Board of Advisors, Bob always gave wise counsel to the Foundation staff when it came to making grants so that the money was used in the most effective way possible. I was very impressed with the two funds he and Jane donated Nov. 25, 2003 of $87,207 each. 1. A Qualified Charitable Gift Annuity. 2. Advise and Consult Fund. These funds have been giving to missions every year. The 12 years he served on the Texas Baptist Missions Foundation, giving and involvement in starting new churches, giving for bicycles for Mexican pastors, giving and trips he made to the border to saturate the community with Bibles, giving and leading prayer groups for the disaster at West, Texas. He made a big donation through the Baptist Men's Brotherhood. He supported every ministry that reported at every meeting of the board, and donated to many of them, especially the Children's home. His ministry with the Foundation really sparked the commitment of many others to missions and giving to missions. Jane really got involved, too. The opportunity to walk alongside him over the years has been a great gift from the Lord.

BILL ARNOLD, TEXAS BAPTISTS

3

BILL ARNOLD'S LETTER ANNOUNCING THE MISSION AWARD

August 30, 2017

Dr. Bob Pinder
119 Juniper Berry Trail
Georgetown, TX 78628

Dear Bob,

Each year during the meeting of the Baptist General Convention of Texas, the Texas Baptist Missions Foundation presents special recognitions to individuals and organizations for outstanding mission service.

It is my privilege, on behalf of the Foundation council, to tell you that we would like to honor you with the *Adventurer Award/for Leadership in Missions*. The recognition is presented each year to an organization or individual in Texas whose leadership has allowed us to take a giant step forward in the task of reaching Texas for Christ. Without a doubt, you fit that description.

The Foundation Council and I have felt that, while institutions have long recognized those who have helped further the cause of the institution, there has not been appropriate recognition of individuals and organizations whose service, leadership and creativity in missions have served as an inspiration and challenge to those who follow in their steps. It is not that they are involved in the task of missions for such recognition, but certainly the story of their accomplishments serves as an inspiration and a challenge to others who must climb the same mountain. That is the way we get missions done — some blaze new trails, others rally the forces behind them and still others stay the course day after day after day.

With that as a background, the Texas Baptist Missions Foundation has established three awards — the *Adventurer Award/or Leadership in Missions,* the *Pioneer Award/or Service in Missions,* and the *Innovator Award/or Creativity in Missions.* These awards will be given annually and, we believe, the legacy of those who receive them will provide a great challenge for the work still to be done. I can think of no better individual in Texas to receive the *Adventurer Award* than Bob Pinder.

My good friend, Don Cramer, made the presentation of the Missions Leadership Award, at the Waco convention.

DR. ROBERT PINDER -ADVENTURER AWARD FOR LEADERSHIP IN MISSIONS

INTRODUCTION

I met Bob in 1999 while on the staff of the Missions Foundation, and we've been good friends ever since Bob's pastor, Jim Haskell of FBC, Georgetown, recommended Bob as a board member. His first activity as a board member was to coordinate a fundraising dinner at his church to help build a new Baptist Student Ministry building at Texas A&M.

SALVATION & MINISTRY

- *Bob's faith journey began at age 10.*
- *He sensed God's call to ministry through his church's youth ministry, where God planted a seed that everyone needed the Lord*
- *He was active in BSU at Stetson University*
- *He became a pastor at age 19*
- *His first baptism was in the cold waters of the Suwannee River, where 18 were baptized*
- *He attended Southern Baptist Seminary in Louisville, Ky.*
- *He pastored 17 years in Florida*
- *Then spent 8 years in Argentina as an IMB missionary, where he started 4 churches.*

TURNING POINT IN HIS MINISTRY

- *While on furlough, Bob then felt led to further his education and focus on ministry to families*
- *He got his PhD at Florida State in 1971, and then spent the next 23 years as Professor of Human Development and Family Studies at Texas Tech University.*
  - *He had a strong ministry with students at Tech*
  - *Leading many to faith in Jesus Christ, and many more to commitment to Christian Ministry*
  - *Bob served as Spiritual advisor to five Christian organizations on campus*
    And he served for years on the BSM committee in the Lubbock Baptist Association

In addition to being a full-time tenured professor at Tech and highly involved in campus life…

Bob had a full-time counseling practice in Lubbock

And led many marriage enrichment retreats and family life conferences

RETIREMENT

Bob decided to move to Sun City in Georgetown to retire

He served a year as chaplain at the Provident Crossings Retirement home

He later started a worship service and served for a year and half as Chaplain at the Oaks retirement home, where he preached every Sunday

At FBC, Georgetown:

> *He served as deacon for 20 plus years*
>
> *He taught a large SS class*
>
> *He attended many mission trips*
>
> *He taught a personal evangelism class*
>
> *He spent 12 years on the Missions Foundation Board*
>
> *He is a founding member of the World Connect special research Board for Missions*
>
> *And he recently pledged a lead gift toward a new Baptist Student Ministry building at Texas Tech, which will be named in his honor*

QUESTIONS

- *What was the most rewarding experience of your ministry?*
  - **"Starting 4 churches in Argentina, and training 6 young deacons how to share their faith"**
- *How would you summarize your life and ministry?*
  - **"Seeing people come to know Jesus and maturing in Christian ministry has been my greatest joy"**

CONCLUSION Bob can definitely look back on his life and say, **"Life Is An Adventure"**

Chapter Two

FRIENDS WHO KNEW ME WELL

My family, friends, and former students have encouraged me to write my life story. I have over thirty current testimonies scattered throughout the book. I had hundreds of letters and notes from students, faculty, and friends, and I make reference to some of them in various sections.

Let me begin with two people who probably know me as well as anybody. Don Cramer is one of my closest friends to this day. He got me involved in the Texas Baptist Missions Foundation Board. Later I will share some of the 12 years of great mission involvement and experiences serving on that board. I also worked with Don when he was Vice President of the Texas Baptist Children's Home. I knew his first wife well and he and Judy are special friends of ours now. Don has helped me tremendously in Estate planning. This is his testimony...

<u>Don Cramer's Testimony</u>
Bob Pinder is, without a doubt, one of the most positive, upbeat, joyful Christians that I have ever known. I do not remember a time when he was not smiling or laughing or at least praising God for his faithfulness when facing heartache or genuine concern over a loved one.

Bob's former pastor, Jim Haskell, introduced me to Bob and suggested that he would make a good board member for the Texas Baptist Missions Foundation, where I served as Vice President from 1997 to 2001. One of my first fundraising projects at TBMF was raising $1.8 Million to build a new Baptist Student Center near the campus of Texas A&M. Bob had been an active supporter of the BSM while serving on the faculty of Texas Tech. In spite of Bob's Red Raider allegiance, he volunteered to host a dinner at FBC, Georgetown and invited all his Aggie friends and others to hear about the Aggie BSM and encourage them to support the project. Bob was also a generous contributor.

Bob's Christian education and service as a pastor, missionary, professor and leader undergirded his passion for missions' advancement across the street and around the world. He graciously accepted my invitation to serve on the TBMF board, and was vocal and financial leader in support of many, many mission projects over the years.

When I returned to Round Rock to again serve on the staff of Texas Baptist Children's Home and the Children At Heart Ministries family, Bob began supporting its expanding ministries to children and families in crisis. His many roles in speaking, teaching and counseling students and adults and families over the years, also gave me a passion for helping children who have experienced abuse and neglect and family crises. I have also watched Bob serve his local community in many church ministries and as chaplain at a local nursing home.

Bob has truly inspired and encouraged me to live life on purpose, even in retirement. Serving God is the greatest privilege in the world at any age and for as long as He gives us breath. Bob has modeled that for me, and I will always be grateful. When asked what was the greatest of all the commandments, Jesus said, *"Love the Lord your God with all your heart and with all your soul and with all your mind....And second is like it: Love your neighbor as yourself."* Our relationship with God and with others is the essence of life....THE most important thing....and Bob's life is witness that Bob gets it! Thanks Bob, for bringing Jesus' words to life! DON CRAMER

Jonathan and Mitzi Ziegner have been special friends for many years, beginning when they were both students at Texas Tech University, and continuing to this day. Mitzi took every course I taught and served as a teaching assistant in my marriage class. Jonathan, an Engineering student, worked for me in my rental property business. He was the best I ever had. He had worked with his dad who owned rental property, and in the summers with his grandfather who built houses. In addition to helping with my rental property, he built a large workshop in my back yard with 10 electrical outlets. We developed a deep friendship. Mitzi tells the story in her testimony...

September 8, 2017 MITZI ZIEGNER'S TESTIMONY
It is hard to articulate just how much of a blessing and an influence Robert Pinder has been in our

*lives, our marriage and my career. I met Dr. Pinder
as an undergraduate student in the mid-1990s in
the Texas Tech College of Human Sciences when
I was a Human Development and Family Studies
student. His class, Early Years of Marriage, had a
reputation for being a favorite and was held in the
college's largest lecture hall, room 169, to a packed
house. Dr. Pinder's magnetic personality and fun,
no-nonsense approach made his class my favorite
each week. He asked me to be his undergraduate
teaching assistant the following semester, and one
day in class asked if anyone knew a "handyman"
that he could hire to work on his rental property. I
recommended the young man I was seriously dating
at the time, Jonathan Ziegner, and the rest, as they
say, is history. Jonathan became Dr. Pinder's "right
hand man" and we grew closer to him and his wife
Jane as our relationship advanced and Jonathan
and I eventually became engaged. Knowing Dr.
Pinder was an ordained minister in addition to
being a professor, we asked him to complete our
pre-marital counseling and to perform our wedding
ceremony. He said he had "retired from doing wed-
dings", but would make an exception for us, and we
were overjoyed. He traveled to Hobbs, New Mexico,
the weekend of July 29, 1995 and performed the
most personal, love filled and precious wedding
alongside the person He chose for me to live out
His plans and purpose for my life.*

*Today, I have the great honor and privilege of
teaching in and serving as the Associate Chair for
the same department of Human Development and*

Family Studies where things all started for me as a student. To this day, I pattern much of my teaching after Dr. Pinder's class. I try to provide a warm and caring environment for my university students, to treat them with compassion and respect and hold them to a high yet reasonable standard. I have no doubt in my mind we would not be where we are today without the lessons Dr. Pinder taught us and the prayers he has, I know, prayed for us throughout the years. In the early years of our marriage we kept in great contact with Dr. Pinder and even visited him and Jane in Georgetown a few times. As time went on and we became busier with our lives, had children and built our careers, we lost touch with the Pinders for a time, but I always thought of them fondly and wondered about how they were doing. Last fall, under the direction of our new Senior Pastor at Lakeridge United Methodist Church, Lyndol Loyd, who I had learned was also an HDFS program graduate and one of Dr. Pinder's former students, we studied a book called The Ten Second Rule about our willingness to be obedient to the Holy Spirit when we feel it. I had a strong feeling during that study that I should reach out to Dr. Pinder and let him know what a blessing and an influence he had been to me. I tracked his daughter Mary down on Facebook, and she helped me get Dr. Pinder's phone number so we could get back in contact. This summer, we were able to meet as a family for lunch as he and his lovely second wife, Joyce, whom he married a few years after losing dear Jane, came through Lubbock on their way to Ruidoso. The prayer he prayed over lunch that day brought tears of gratitude to my eyes. The opportunity to see Dr. Pinder again, introduce him to our children and let him see the family that grew from the marriage ceremony he performed was the richest of blessings and such a reminder of how very good God is. Jonathan and I will always, always love Dr. Pinder and be grateful the Lord placed him in our lives and made him a part of our story. When I think of this precious man, the song "Thank You for Giving to the Lord" by Ray Boltz comes to mind. Jonathan and I are indeed lives that were changed.

With deepest love, God's grace and so much gratitude, Mitzi and Jonathan Ziegner

My Christian Testimony

I had a strong Christian influence in my classes, across the campus, and throughout all of Lubbock and West Texas. I preached in nearly every Baptist Church in the area, including three long term interim pastorates. Other details are scattered throughout the book. The aspect of my ministry that thrills me the most is the number of students who surrendered to the Lord for vocational Christian service. Two of those couples are serving in Christian ministries on Tech's campus today.

Jeff and Paige Kennon were both students of mine. Jeff has been serving as the Director of the Baptist Student Ministry at Texas Tech since 2007. God has richly blessed his ministry all these years.

13

Jeff's Testimony

I walked on to the campus of Texas Tech University in 1985 with the intent of getting a pre-law degree. As is the custom for many students however, my plans changed. I decided that God had gifted me and was therefore calling me into vocational ministry. I didn't know what all that meant at the time, but it led me to meet Dr. Robert Pinder, who would become one of my main professors towards me getting a Human Development/Family Studies degree. I'm pretty sure I took every class he taught.

His classes were always favorites of mine, and it wasn't because I got A's in all of them. Dr. Pinder actually cared about his students. For him, teaching was bigger than just delivering content, it was about investing in others. I'll have to admit that I don't remember all that he taught in class. In fact, I probably wouldn't be able to pass one of his tests today. But the one thing I have not forgotten was Dr. Pinder, his character, and his willingness to serve students at Texas Tech.

It hasn't been until recently that our paths have crossed again. This is due to his willingness to invest in a new building for the Baptist Student Ministry at Texas Tech of which I am the director. When I first heard of Dr. Pinder's desire to give the naming gift for our new building, I was overwhelmed, but not necessarily surprised. And as I continue to hear about the impact that Dr. Pinder has made on college students throughout the years and his continued love for them, it is no wonder why his generosity is aimed towards insuring that future generations of Tech students will have an opportunity to hear the gospel.

Dr. Pinder has been faithful to what God has called him to be and as a result, I, along with many others, have been taught, encouraged, and shown an example of what it means to follow and share Christ throughout one's life. Blessings to you Dr. Pinder!!!

Jeff Kennon

Trace Hunt married after graduating from Tech. He met Christina in Cristian ministry. After their marriage, they became missionaries with Cru, the North American arm of the Campus Crusade for Christ mission. In 2007 they were appointed to serve on the campus of Texas Tech University. This is Trace's testimony.

Trace's Testimony

I recently came across some old notes from a college class. It's a wonder I hadn't thrown this away. As I flipped through my notes on "The Early Years of Marriage" by Dr. Robert Pinder, I had a flood of memories. My first two years in college were a roller coaster ride of confusion, both educationally and relationally. My junior year was the big turnaround. I had recently given my life to Christ at a Campus Crusade conference and had changed my major for the 2nd time. This time, however, I discovered Dr. Pinder, a man after God's own heart. In a university where very few professors are believers, to find one so open and bold in his Christian faith was life giving to me. I took every class he taught and even became his Teacher's Assistant for every class he taught. I majored in "Pinder" and it changed the trajectory of my life. My wife and I just celebrated 25 years of marriage and 24 years as missionaries with Cru, the US ministry of Campus Crusade for Christ. Dr. Pinder was a gift from above and it's no wonder I never threw away my notes. I'm still practicing the things he taught us.

Trace Hunt
Cru Missionary
Texas Tech University

This week I received this email of two students from different years who did not know each other and made contact through an article written about me in the HDFS alumni paper.

My sweet Dr. Pinder,

If you only knew the number of times I've said, "Thanks to Dr. Pinder I've been able to...." You made such a mark on me during my time at Tech. Thank you. But the real mark has been the years after–30 years ago last May I graduated from TTU–I have built a wonderful life in Midland. You gave me the confidence and education to take on amazing, challenging, make a difference work over the years. Thank you.

I am also happy to say that Danny and I will celebrate 30 years of marriage on October 22. Thanks to your amazing marriage skills classes–you've made a difference in the home life too.

I loved reading about you in the latest e-newsletter from the HDFS college. Praise–all deserved my sweet man.

Mitzi and I are finding we share so much–I am so blessed to have her in my life and Tech is so lucky to have her leading and teaching the future.
I had to reach out to you and say, "thank you!"

Much love-
*Carla Higley Holeva–*Class of 1988 HDFS

I love Dr. Pinder dearly too, Carla...I also took several classes with him and was his undergrad TA. Another fun fact is that he is an ordained minister and actually preformed our wedding ceremony 23 years ago. He also had rental property when he was a TTU faculty member, and my now husband (finance at the time) worked part time for him doing maintenance and repair work on those houses and duplexes while we were undergrads. Love that we are connected in this way, and I am still in touch with Dr. Pinder, so including him on this email so that you can be, too. I will second all Carla's words and say that our marriages are just two of I know what must be countless others that have been positively impacted by your teaching, Dr. Pinder. I'm so grateful the Lord was able to use you in such a mighty way during your time at TTU. You have changed the trajectory of lives, careers marriages and families in more ways than you'll ever realize, Dr. Pinder, and you are a man dearly and deeply loved!

Thanks for including me in this response, Carla... we do indeed share so much and I'm very grateful to have gotten acquainted with you!

MITZI ZEIGNER

This is the TT College of Human Sciences article that brought Mitzi and Carla together.

Robert "Bob" Pinder Honored with Naming of TTU Student Ministry Building

Former Human Development and Family Studies (HDFS) professor, Robert "Bob" Pinder, Ph.D., recently celebrated both his 90th birthday and the news of a student ministry building located just off the Texas Tech University campus to be named in his honor.

With many years as an HDFS professor, Dr. Pinder's impact is still remembered long after his retirement. Dr. Pinder taught HDFS courses in the College of Human Sciences from 1971 to 1994 where he received tenure and was on the graduate school faculty. Dr. Pinder taught the first course in Family Therapy, which has grown to become one of today's leading academic fields.

Dr. Pinder was known for his enthusiasm for recruiting students to Human Development and Family Studies and Texas Tech University.

Current HDFS Professor Jean Scott, Ph.D., remembers her former colleague as a very congenial and pleasant individual. She recalls that Dr. Pinder was well known in the department for several popular undergraduate and graduate courses that he taught, particularly the courtship and marriage course.

"I remember meeting people who were Tech graduates and when I would tell them that I was a faculty member in HDFS, they would often name the courtship and marriage course as one they really enjoyed and found useful. Dr. Pinder really cared for the students who took his courses."

HDFS alumnus, Jeff Kennon, reflects on his time as a Red Raider with many courses taught by Dr. Pinder.

"I'm pretty sure I took every class he taught. His classes were always favorites of mine, and it wasn't because I got A's in all of them. Dr. Pinder actually cared about his students. For him, teaching was bigger than just delivering content, it was about investing in others."

Since leaving Texas Tech, Dr. Pinder continued to lead a life filled with teaching alongside his late wife of 60 years, Jane. Bob later met his now wife, Joyce, and married her in 2012. The couple now resides in a retirement home together where he says they are doing great.

Dr. Pinder is working on his life story, to be published soon with many memories of his Texas Tech days and lifetime of teaching and ministry. As a longtime friend of the Texas Tech Baptist Student Ministry, Dr. Pinder was awarded the Texas Baptist Adventurer in Missions Award last year. Today, the organization is honoring him with the new building namesake.

Chapter Three

BUT LET'S START FROM THE BEGINNING...

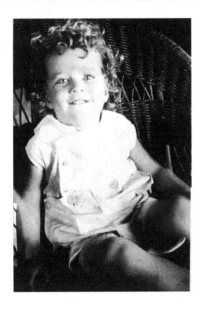

Dr. ROBERT HENRY PINDER

This is my story.

I was born February 5, 1928 in Miami, Florida to William Comfort Pinder and Wilhelmina Folk Pinder. I was the middle of three boys. William Comfort, Jr, Bill, was three years older than I. Walter Folk, Walt, was 18 months younger. We were poor but did not know it nor talk about it. We learned early that there were limited resources so we never asked for anything. Dad worked hard. It was the depression and he worked for the WPA, government work when he had no work. He was a railroad conductor all his working years for the Florida East Coast Railroad, until it went into receivership and he retired. We never had much interaction with him until his retirement. I remember seeing him go off to work and going to bed. There may have been more that I just don't remember.

Mom was a stay at home mom, always available and attentive to our needs. We had no car and depended on walking, bicycles and buses and street cars. Bill was sort of a loner. Walt and I were very close and did everything together. We went to each other's church socials, and shared many of the same friends. We spent most of our time playing with the neighbors in the street. We ran boards from tree to tree in a vacant lot and ran around like monkeys up in the trees. One day Walt tried to hold on to a board and swing down. He lost his grip and went soaring into the air. He landed on his back and had the air knocked out of him. I thought sure he was dead and did what I could until he started breathing. A boy who had no siblings lived next door. He had lots of toys and we made good use of them, usually with his permission. We played games like kick the can, hide and seek, etc. until mom called us in for dinner by playing the song beginning the Lone Ranger program on the radio real loud at our front door.

We walked to school every day. Actually we ran most of the way because we were running late. Bill was the intellectual in the family and read and studied a lot. Walt and I just got by, but we never failed any subjects. Walt and I learned to swim at the YMCA pool. We played all kinds of sports at the city park programs. I was a school safety patrol boy and won a city wide award for my work. I played the violin and was "first chair" in the Junior High orchestra until I made the basketball team. You had to weigh 100 pounds to play. I had a hard time, eating bananas, etc. to get up to 100 pounds. In High School I played all sports. Basketball was always my favorite. I was captain of the team my senior year. We went all the way across town, passing other high schools in order to attend Miami Senior High because it had the best teams. We won the State championship nearly every year. I learned to work early. Before I was old enough to have a paper route, I sold papers on a street corner. I sold a magazine called "Liberty" and made money but also coupons which I used to buy my first bicycle. Later I had a paper route. I also worked in a department store, and folded the Sunday paper about all night Saturday night at the Miami Herald. Later I worked at an airplane factory, making tail assemblies for P38 government airplanes.

I did very little dating. There was no money nor time for that. What few dates I had were by bicycle and bus. But we had plenty of social life, playing spin the bottle at church socials. Whoops, Mom did not know about that. A group of about 100 from our high school would meet at Miami Beach about 20 miles away almost every Saturday. What fun. I got to running around with six guys who were not a good influence. We started out stealing reflectors off the license tags of cars. I had a big box of those hidden under my bed. Later they started stealing bicycles and repainting them. The Lord was gracious to me. He yanked me out of that group, sent me back to our church youth group and through those experiences God called me to the ministry. Bill was very critical of my decision and said, you will never make a preacher. David Mashburn, our Educational Director at church and Dr. C. Roy Angell, my pastor, took me under their wing. They said, Bob if God has called you, then you need to start and they planned for me to speak at Prayer meeting on Wednesday night. I did terribly, Bill would not let me forget it. But Mr. Mashburn wouldn't quit. After high school I went to Stetson University, a Baptist school to study for the ministry. That is when my life really blossomed. God gave me all kinds of experiences for Spiritual, social, and intellectual growth.

We used to spend every summer in South Carolina where Mom was born and had lots of brothers and sisters and other family. I thought we must be rich to live in Miami in the winter and South Carolina in the summer. It was much later that I found out that Dad had good work on the railroad in the winter when all of the Yankees came to Florida but was on the "extra board" and irregular work in the summer. As a railroad employee we got a family pass and we could travel free, so to survive, Mom took all three boys to the country. We split up staying at various homes and working in the crops and really enjoyed our cousins and a different lifestyle. The homes did not have electricity. We got water from pumps or wells. Anything at night was done by kerosene lamps. Cooking was done on a big wood burning stove. Clothes were washed in a big iron kettle, heated by wood fire in the yard and hung on fences and lines across the yard to dry. Ironing was done with solid irons heated in the fireplace or on the stove. The toilet was an outhouse, usually a two seater, supplied with a Sears catalog, or anywhere behind trees. We bathed, using a #2 wash tub behind the fig tree. At night there was a big pot under the bed. Life was challenging but lots of fun.

We went to church in a horse drawn wagon or buggy. One Sunday I had the reigns and somebody said, "Bob, we need to go faster." I hit the horse, he jumped and Aunt Stella who was sitting on the back of the wagon with her legs hanging out, landed in the middle of the road. No air conditioning. Heated by a big stove in the middle of the church. Lighted by kerosene lamps around the walls, brought by members. We played with cars which were big match boxes in the house and old bottles in the yard. "People" were cut outs from the Sears and Roebuck catalog. Most of the cousins were girls. That is where we, boys, learned about girls. There was no television, only radio. Uncle Herbert, one of mom's brothers, was deaf and I learned the hand alphabet to be able to communicate with him. He was my favorite. His wife, Mozelle, later on ran a boarding house when they moved into town. She loaded the table with about three meats and thirty vegetables and salads every noon. Conversation included some really interesting people. All of mom's family were Christians, some more devout than others.

Aunt Stella, a widow, was a saint. She had Sunbeams at her house and that started my interest and commitment to missions. She had the whole world on her heart with great compassion. Her son, Robert, was one of my favorite cousins. When it was time for us to return to Miami, he would ask," Are you going back to your-ami, (Miami)." They would plant tomato plants near the woods where we cut stove wood. We would take water, salt, and biscuits and cut fire wood and eat tomato sandwiches for lunch. We worked all of the crops wherever we were staying, mostly I stayed with Uncle Herbert. We would load up a truck and take watermelons to Columbia, about 60 miles away and sell them on the streets. Lunch was canned Vienna sausages and a moon pie. We would sack up small bags of boiled peanuts and take them to town (Bamberg) on Saturday and sell them on the street. What little I would make, was enough for candy and the picture show. A big treat was to buy a banana. What fun we had. We would have big family get togethers and eat and talk. What stories we heard. Some of these were boiled peanut parties, cooked in the big kettle in the yard used for washing clothes. Some were fish fries fried in the same kettle. The hush puppies were as good as the fish. Some were sugar cane grindings and cooking into syrup.

We had some of the greatest revivals in those churches. Usually they ended with a big dinner on the grounds with enough food to feed the whole community. Lemonade was made in a big tank. At one revival, Walt left the church and was sitting in a pickup truck in the parking lot and accidentally the horn started blowing and wouldn't stop. The preacher said that's the devil blowing that horn. Walt never forgot that. Dad and Bill were baptized after one of those revivals. Dad would go with us on occasion to church, but mostly it was mom and us boys. Dad became a serious Christian after I surrendered to the ministry. During my college days I was asked to be one of the speakers at Ridgecrest student week, about 2000 college students in North Carolina. Mom and Dad went with me. One day dad pulled me aside and said, "Bob, teach me how to pray." After retirement dad became really devout. He wouldn't miss church and was a tither, and would pray in public. It brought much joy to all of us, especially mom. Mom was one of the best, strongest Christians I have ever known. It was 24 hours a day, 7/365 a year in every situation. She was never hard on us boys but we knew where she stood on every issue. Whenever we left the house, she would say "Be as sweet as you look" and then spent most of the time on her knees until we returned.

Dad's brother was a drunk and gambler. We seldom saw him. One day he brought alcohol to the house and mom ordered him out of the house in her calm but stern way. Dad's stepfather was a drunk. He had to live with us for several years. He never drank in the house but was drunk most of the time. I am sure it was terrible for mom but she put up with him and showed such compassion for him. It was her strong Christian life that showed all of us that being a Christian was the only way to live.

RIDGECREST BAPTIST ASSEMBLY

I spent four summers on the staff at the Ridgecrest Baptist Assembly. I was co-employed at the Boy's Camp owned and operated by the assembly, and on the assembly staff. I was a lifeguard at the lake used by the assembly and I also taught swimming, life-saving, diving and was a life guard at the boy's camp. I also taught basketball and other sports, hiking, and other activities. The camp counselors and other assembly staff played competitive basketball with other assemblies and camps in that part of North Carolina.

A tragic event happened one summer. There were six of us life-guards at the lake. Often we would have hundreds of youth from the Assembly swimming and using the canoes. One day we were informed that a boy went swimming and never returned to the hotel. We found his clothes hanging on a tree limb. He was alone and must have dived into the lake and never resurfaced. We got hooks and dragged the lake until we hooked his body and pulled him into the boat. It was a big shock and sad experience. His family were wonderful Christians and never blamed us. We all attended his funeral.

College students working at the Assembly cleaned the hotel rooms, worked in the dining room, worked in all of the stores, and all activities of the Assembly. We were organized like a BSM organization on a college campus. The fellowship was great. That is where I first met Jane but we never dated until years later. She graduated one year ahead of me and taught school in Ocala, Fl. where her brother, Scott, had a dental practice. She often came swimming during staff swimming times. She and a girl-friend took a canoe one day and overturned it in the lake. That was a pretty common experience. I went out to upright the canoe and help them get back in. In the accident Jane lost the top of her bathing suit and I retrieved it for her.

One year polio was epidemic in Florida. The camp director asked me to set up an auxiliary camp in a nearby lodge for 15 boys coming from Florida who had to be quarantined for three weeks before they could move into the Boys camp. That was a challenge but a fun experience. I, alone, had the full responsibility of the group 24 hours a day for three weeks, for everything except meals. I threatened to send home any boy who caused any problems and that settled it. They were a good bunch of kids and we quickly bonded and had a great time. I kept them occupied with all kinds of activities, especially hiking in the mountains. They were so tired at night they were ready for bed.

The six life guards really bonded. On our day off we travelled all over, especially Ashville about 18 miles away. We enjoyed a show and a chocolate sundae. Just 3 miles away was Black Mountain and 2 miles up the mountain from there was Montreet, where Billy Graham had a home. There was also a girls camp there and when allowed we really enjoyed that trip. One weekend we went to Wilmington, NC on the coast where one of the lifeguards was from. His mom really made us feel at home. He had an old ford car that we all enjoyed. It would not make sharp turns so going down the mountain we often had to skid around the curves. Talk about excitement.

One Summer I worked for the Home Mission Board, thinking they would send me someplace exciting like Alaska or Hawaii. They sent me 300 miles to Ybor city, Tampa, Fla to work with two old maids in a Good Will Center. I had a great Summer and it enhanced my experience and desire for mission work. We ministered to people with all kinds of needs, poverty, physical handicaps, broken homes, and every kind of relationship problems. God taught me many things, especially patience and listening skills.

Chapter Four

MY COLLEGE YEARS

A fter I made my decision for the ministry, it was just assumed that I would go to college. I had made application to go to Georgia Tech because my grades and all of the high school tests indicated I ought to be an engineer. After my decision for the ministry, my pastor suggested that I should consider Stetson University, the Baptist University in Florida. I would get financial aid and better preparation for the ministry. When it was time to go, I packed a small bag, walked to the corner, and took a bus to the train station. My dad worked for the Florida East Coast Railroad. Using our family pass, I took the train to New Smyrna, and hitch hiked to DeLand, where Stetson is located. I went through the registration all on my own. I looked around and nearly everyone had their parents with them to register. My years at Stetson were some of the best years of my life.

I was assigned a roommate in a private home near the campus. He was John Bray who had been an evangelist for eight years before returning to college to complete his degree. John was a really nice guy, but was extreme in his religious beliefs. He had written books on dancing, smoking, drinking, and things he thought were most important. We had a lot of differences in our beliefs.

I jumped right into being active in the Baptist Student Union. (BSU). The activities of the BSU became my major in college. The

Director took me under his wing and encouraged me in all kinds of ministry. I would preach six times at various cells at the city jail every Sunday. One of the jobs I had was working in the school cafeteria. Three black ladies who worked with me became good friends. One day they asked me if I would preach at their women's missionary meeting. I was anxious to preach. I immediately said yes, thinking it would be a small group of very encouraging people. I arrived at the church to find it packed. Six black pastors were lined up to usher me in. An elderly pastor could tell I was nervous. He whispered to me, don't be nervous, just say a good word for Jesus. That relaxed me and I was able to preach. The "AMENS" kept me going.

The house where I lived was an upstairs apartment. Dotson and Betty Mills, good friends from Miami, lived on the first floor. Two of my friends lived with me and the second year my brother, Walt, joined me. David Thomas, one of my friends was pastor of a church near Gainesville. He recommended me as pastor to the Priscilla Baptist Church. I was 19 years old and thrilled to pastor my own church. I was very evangelistic. All I knew to do was go from farm to farm witnessing. The first time I baptized, I baptized 18 in Blue Spring, a cold spring that fed into the Suwannee River.

8-07-49 – Pastor Robert (Bob) Pinder, John Bass Jr., Clara Bass, L.J. Bass, Derwood Bryant, Mrs. John (Anne Mae) Davis, Mr. John Davis, J.W. Davis, Bryant Davis, Monroe Davis, Daniel Jenkins, Vassie Jones Jr., Lavenne Johnson, J.D. Johnson, Jo Anne Mathis, Maxie McCullough, Peggy Rolling, Vernon Rolling, Roy Wilson

A wonderful family, the Bryants, adopted me and I stayed with then every Saturday night. They had two girls and a five year old boy, Charles, I called him BoPeep. After Joyce and I married, I received a call from Houston. BoPeep had heard that I was in Texas and he was determined to find me. He and his wife, Anita, came and visited us. He brought a framed picture of me and the 18 that I baptized. I did not know the picture existed. What a surprise.

Charles wrote me recently, recalling all of these experiences and also a Sunday "when we were headed for church in a bad thunderstorm. The roads were in bad shape, mud puddles all over. The car was stuck in mud. Some of the men got out to push the car. Brother Bob got out, rolled up his pants, and helped push. That really impressed me that a preacher would do something like that."

I did not know that the church had an annual call. I had a great ministry there but the people were accustomed to an older pastor who would live in the area. I went to preach one Sunday and Mrs. Bryant, my adopted mother said, come by the house after church tonight. I told her I had an exam the next day and needed to hurry home. She said, you must come by. She asked me, did you know that was your last sermon in this church. I was devastated.

I had become good friends with my religion professor, Dr. Lafayette Walker. I went to his office Monday morning and cried like a baby. I thought if I cannot be successful at this little country church, then maybe I was not meant to be a preacher. He assured me that was not the case. He sent me to preach at a large church the next Sunday. Then the following Sunday, he sent me to the First Baptist Church in Mims, Fl., near Cape Canaveral on the coast. They were looking for a pastor. They called me and I had a wonderful ministry there until I graduated from college.

31

They wanted me to stay on permanently after graduation. I visited again with Dr. Walker. I trusted his council. He said, Bob, you have had a great ministry at Mims. The church has grown tremendously and there is a sweet spirit in the church. There is no doubt that you could have a great ministry there for many years. But, if you stay on at that church, you probably would never go to the Seminary and continue your education. I took his advice, resigned the church, and went to Southern Baptist Seminary in Louisville, Ky, to continue my education.

There was an interesting experience at the Priscilla church, and may have influenced the church to decide this young preacher is too much of a challenge and change. They had always used two glasses, (actually, two canning jars), for the communion service. After the bread, they would pass the glasses down the rows with the wine. It was very unsanitary and I knew the congregation wanted to change. At the next business meeting I suggested ordering the tray of individual glasses. Uncle Zack was chairman of the deacons and in charge of preparing the elements for communion, like his father before him. Do you see the pattern? He got up and made a strong speech. He said that Jesus took THE CUP, one cup, and we should follow his example. I said, Uncle Zack, we have been using two glasses. The vote was unanimous but Uncle Zack abstained. I knew the cups we ordered had arrived and were stored behind the piano. I confirmed that with him. The next time for communion I came out from teaching a class and saw the table covered and ready for the service. I had a brief message and he and I took our positions at each end of the table. As we lifted the cloth, I saw that he had prepared the table like always, with the two jars. I did not react but went ahead with the service. I asked Uncle Zack to go with me behind the church. I said the church voted to use the individual glasses. He said it was against his beliefs and he could not serve it that way. I said let's get your son to take over. He agreed and his son did a good job, but I think Uncle Zack never forgave me. Traditions are hard to change.

My life in college was full and fulfilling. I pastored a church all four years of my college career. I had three part time jobs, working in the school cafeteria, the post office, and a laundry route. Still, I was very active on campus. I did not have the time nor the money to join a fraternity, but I was welcomed in all of the fraternity and sorority houses. I was on the Hatter staff, and Religion Editor on the Stetson Reporter, writing a weekly Christian article. I was an officer in the BSU every year, and active in all their activities. I was Promotional Director of the State BSU. I was the preacher on the State BSU Youth Revival team, preaching 13 revivals one Summer from Miami to Pensacola. Bill Holley was the soloist/music leader on the team. He had a beautiful Tenor voice. After graduation, he studied and performed for years in Austria and Germany. I remembered that he was from Blountstown, a small town in west Florida. I called him recently. He could not write anything for my book because of his dementia. We recalled many of the interesting experiences of those revivals.

One of those revivals was in the Ancient City Baptist Church, the largest church in Saint Augustine, Florida. There were a number of people who were saved the first three nights of the Revival and the Pastor decided to have a baptismal service on Wednesday night. After dinner we hurried back to the church so Bill could rehearse with the choir. When we arrived at the church, some of the youth told us the theme banner over the choir loft had fallen. I told Bill to meet with the choir and I would fix the banner. The auditorium was pitch dark and I felt my way down the aisle. I knew the light switches were on the left edge of the platform. I did not know that the baptistery was an opening in the floor of the platform. I stepped onto the platform and took one step into the baptistery. The choir heard the splash and immediately I was surrounded with 50 young people. I did own another suit. When I arrived back at the church, the service was under way and the congregation informed of the details. I asked Bill to let me take a moment to explain and let them laugh it out so we could continue in worship. For years that was a state wide story at all Baptist Convention meetings.

PREACHER for a Youth Revival at Riverside Baptist Church at 8 p. m. Sunday through Friday will be the Rev. Bob Pinder (above) Bill Holley to serve as song leader. "Christ the Way" is the theme for the revival, in charge of State Baptist Student Union Youth Team.

I was an officer in the ministerial association every year, and president my senior year. I was elected to the Press club, Ye Mystic Krewe, an honorary fraternity, the honor roll, and the travel squad of the glee club. My senior year I was voted by the student body as one of the 20 most popular students on campus, with a full page picture in my senior annual.

In my freshman year I noticed that there were a lot of students from Miami, so I organized a Stetson Miami Club. Jeanne Bieggers, a beautiful girl, Orange Bowl Queen, was in the club and we started dating. After a few dates I could tell she was a party girl and would never fit my call to the ministry, so I broke up with her. She was so heartbroken (Joke) that she dropped out of school. Maybe she flunked out. She did not know who Dean Martin was but attended one of his concerts in Miami Beach. He flirted with her all night, and she followed him all over the country and broke up his marriage. They married in 1949, my junior year. She was his favorite wife. They were married for 24 years and had three children. I saw that she died recently at 89 years of age.

Chapter Five

MY SEMINARY YEARS

After graduation I went to Southern Baptist Seminary in Louisville, Ky. and Jane went to Crestview and taught school, living at home. We planned on getting married after that year. I had already committed to being the BSU Youth evangelist that summer, preaching in 13 revivals all over the state.

We thought we would get married after I completed the revivals and go directly to Louisville. When my schedule came in, I had a month after I finishing my year at the Seminary before my first revival and the last revival left just a week for us to get to Louisville, so we got married at the first of the summer and had a nice honeymoon at Ridgecrest, NC. After the last revival we went to Louisville and we both went full time as students. I got two masters in three more years and Jane got her Masters in Religious Education.

We both had saved about $1,000 each and decided we would both get a Seminary education. We felt that was God's will for us and that He would provide the way. We had a single+ room in the seminary dormitory. My good friends, Bill and Barbara Guess had a room down the hall. We had a waffle iron and they had an electric cup. We had many meals together by that combination. They continued as great friends until Bill's death. I preached four revivals in different churches he pastored.

My first year in the seminary I developed a deep friendship with Asa Jones who sat beside me in my New Testament class. He recommended me to the First Baptist Church in Graefenburg, Ky. They called me to be their pastor. The committee came to our one room home to confirm the decision of the church. The chairman said the church had authorized them to offer to pay our moving expenses. I said, that won't be necessary, I can put everything we own in the back seat of our car. Jane and I really loved our four years in that church. It was only eight miles from Frankfort the Capitol of Kentucky. There was a great group of young couples in the church that worked at the Capitol. We made several trips and had a lot of fellowship with them. The church had a small house next to the church which became our home for four years.

We drove every day to the seminary for classes. Jane did not have much experience cooking. Her two older sisters helped her mother cook and she and Betty, her younger sister, washed the dishes. I gave her a cook book for a wedding present. She really worked at it and became a wonderful cook. We did have a few of what we called, "burnt offerings". Every Sunday we had lunch at the home of a different family in the church. Families signed up for months in advance and usually invited another family or two to join us. The table was always loaded with the best of country food. That kept us from starving.

Clark Dawson had been the soloist and song leader in the church but years earlier he got his feelings hurt and vowed never to sing in church again. He and I developed a friendship going to Baptist meetings together. I led the singing and I kept asking him to sing a solo. One Sunday he agreed. Not singing for years had left its toll, and he did not sing well. He had strong convictions about everything. I asked him one day what he would be if he was not a Baptist. He said, if I was not a Baptist and a Democrat, I would be ashamed of myself.

A previous pastor had influenced the church to jack up the church building and build a full basement under the church. It leaked terribly. Whenever it rained we had an inch of water on the floor. We opened our home for classes. The house had a cistern as the water supply. The former pastor thought that the water was unsafe for drinking. We drank it for four years with no ill effects.

Mary Jo Brooks added this testimony of 64 years ago. " I belonged and attended Graefenburg Baptist Church at the time you were our pastor, and still attend today. I remember it to be a very good time for the church and also remember Jane being our Choir Director. It was fun and we all loved her very much.

I was the former Mary Jane Kays and I guess the most memorable and wonderful memory of your ministry was that you married Calvin Bolin and me July 16, 1953. It has been 64 years of happiness and we are still together, which is very good. God has truly blessed us with 4 wonderful children and they all trust the Lord. *I think you all left Graefenburg soon afterward, but we have always managed to keep up with you along the way.*

Carrie Bemiss remembers that time in history.

"I remember you and Jane working at Dover Baptist camp one summer and Wilma Kays and I went. I loved that camp. I also know you married Dove and Charles Quire (who had been married before) and the Southern Baptist at that time said you were not supposed to, so Dove remembers. I was around twelve when you all left but have good memories of that time. Hope all is well with you all."

We were very close friends with Elmer and Ginny Dawson in the church at that time. When we moved to Louisville for our last year at the Seminary, we lived above them in an apartment. We kept up with them through the years, and travelled with them and visited in their home. Ginny recently called me and recalled our times together.

I preached a two week Revival in a church in a town about forty miles away. In addition to the nightly evangelistic services, I led Vacation Bible School and preached a morning service every day. The pastor and I visited prospects in the afternoons. We had breakfast, lunch and dinner in different homes. It was challenging to say the least.

I was very evangelistic in college, preaching revivals for many of the students who pastored churches. I was the preacher on the state BSU youth Revival team, preaching thirteen revivals all over the state one Summer. I had to take the required course on the psychology of religion taught by Dr Wayne Oates, a renowned leader in the field of counseling and pastoral care. The first day of classes he said young men to be successful pastors you need to know three things. You need to know the Lord Jesus with a strong born again believers faith and have a testimony like the apostle Paul who said, "I know whom I have believed and I am persuaded that He is able to keep that which I have committed unto him against that day." Secondly, you need to know the Bible and make it your textbook for the rest of your life. Thirdly, you need to know and understand people. You will be interacting with all kinds of people throughout your ministry. He really opened my mind and heart. I took every class he taught.

After we both finished our first degrees, we moved into an apartment near the seminary. Jane taught school while I worked on a second seminary degree. Dr. Oates, my major professor, mentor and friend, invited me and six other graduates to be involved in an intense program. It was an exciting year, working in three hospitals and the state mental hospital. Through the process of that year, he wrote the book, *The Religious Factors in Mental Illness*. He gave us reference in the preface as helping him write the book. He added a new perspective to my ministry. He wanted me to go into the chaplaincy, either hospital or military. I told him I felt called to pastor churches. He said if that is your calling, I want to recommend you to the First Baptist Church in St. Joseph, Louisiana where a former doctoral graduate of mine has been pastor for ten years. They wanted a pastor with the same background.

They called me as pastor and I traveled to the church every third week until I graduated. Jane and I did not have any children and it was a relaxing pastorate. I went fishing and hunting with the men and was active in the local theater group. Jane had friends and activities that kept her occupied. We would make trips to Natchez and Vicksburg Mississippi and to Monroe and other Louisiana cities just to eat out. I visited nearly every family in the area.

After two years I accepted the call of the First Baptist Church in Umatilla, Florida, as pastor. I was considered a community leader. I was President of the Lion's club. They called on me to pray at the opening of the county shuffleboard tournament, etc. While we were there we adopted Cindy, our first child, March 11, 1956. We wanted children so much, Jane asked her mother to see if her doctor could find a child to adopt. We adopted Cindy and took her home when she was one day old. We did not know Cindy's mother's medical history. Cindy was bi-polar and had lots of health and other problems all of her life. She died July 13, 2015. We provided her a home, rent free and her last ten years were the happiest of her life. Her daughter, Rachel, inherited bi-polar but is doing well, teaching school and providing well for her two happy boys.

DUKE HAGOOD'S TESTIMONY

I don't remember how old I was the first time my path crossed my uncle Bob's. But I do know the very first memory I have of him. I will always remember my older brother, John, being amazed that Uncle Bob had the coolest patent leather shoes he had ever seen. It wasn't too long after he had seen them for the first time that both of us ended up with a pair of our own for church and Sunday school. When uncle Bob and aunt Jane lived in Umatilla (40 miles from our home in Ocala), we would sometimes go down to hear him preach at his church and have lunch with them afterward. Being the fashionable trend-setter he was, we Hagood boys always took note of his clothes and shoes. Uncle Bob was the coolest cat around. We always looked forward to our visits!

Through the years as their family grew and Bob and Jane went on the mission field, our times together became much less frequent, but whenever we had the opportunity to be together uncle Bob *was always the most loving, friendly uncle a young nephew could have wanted. He was full of Godly wisdom, and there were times as I was growing up that I <u>definitely</u> needed it!*

He and aunt Jane came to visit Becky and I one time early in our relationship and we loved hearing him talk about marriage and family. Some of what he shared we definitely put into practice. He always encouraged us to set a good example to other couples we were mentoring and discipling within our church.

I remember on one particular visit, he pulled me aside after being around my dad for a few days to talk to me. He'd asked me if I'd noticed the change he'd seen in my dad. I confessed that I hadn't really thought about some of the things he had noticed but he told me that he thought my dad was showing signs of dementia. Several months after this discussion, dad was diagnosed with Alzheimer's. During this hard time, uncle Bob was there for us and told us to be ready to become the caretakers that our parents would need us to be. We were so grateful for his encouragement to our family.

Uncle Bob has always been a prayer warrior and God has certainly blessed him with a long life and good health. He is a lover of Jesus and his Word, and has ministered to all of us through the years. I, for one, am a life impacted and changed by my Uncle Bob's – and I congratulate him on a life well lived and loved.

Chapter Six

CALL TO THE MISSION FIELD

I was called to pastor a large church in Miami, Fl. It was a good church, a real evangelistic opportunity in the Coral Gables area of the big city. Some deacons and I visited prospects two nights weekly. I baptized every Sunday night for three years while I was there. While we were there, Rob was born, September 13, 1958. Judy was born September 6, 1959, just as I was beginning a new pastorate at Hiland Park Baptist Church in Panama City, Fl. Jane went to her mother's home in Crestview, Fl. for the birth. I built a strong church and started a much needed building program. It is a large, megachurch today.

The Executive Secretary of the Florida Baptist Convention and the head of the Evangelism Department called me and asked if I would start a new church in the Orlando area. They said, "Mickey Mouse and secularism is taking over the Orlando area. We need to start more churches and reach more people with the gospel". They knew my history of building churches and starting new churches. They bought a house in a new subdivision and we moved into the house. I began services in the living room of our home. With the support of the First Baptist Church and the new church fund of the convention, we bought land and started a building. It was an evangelistic challenge, starting from scratch. God really blessed our efforts and in three years we had a membership of over 700 members. Though it was a busy pastorate, I took a two hour lunch break. Jane would have a picnic lunch ready and often we would take the boat and the three kids to the local lake. We really enjoyed the lunch, swim, and boating with all the family.

OUR CALL TO THE MISSION FIELD

While I was pastor in Orlando Florida, Baker James Cauthen came for a Statewide Missions Conference. I was on the program and seated on the platform. Jane was in the audience. He made a plea for missionary service. He said our world is hell bound and we cannot wait for young people to respond to the call and get their education and experience. Some of you pastors who are fully pre-pared to go, need to respond. Why not pray this prayer, "I know the world is in need of the Gospel. I am prepared to go. Unless the Lord closes the door or redirects my life, I am going." Jane and I both went home that night convinced that we should apply. We were two years over the age limit. Bill Dyal, my friend from Kentucky days, was working in the area of reviewing the applica-tions. In six months we had finished all of the requirements for appointment and headed for the mission field in Argentina.

The mission Board sent us to Costa Rica for a year of language study. On our flight to Costa Rica Jane told me that she thought she was pregnant. It was confirmed. She had no maternity clothes or any other preparation for the year. We both went to classes all day and had homework at night. We rode the rickety busses to care for our needs. Our three kids were in school and doing well. We had a full time maid to cook and clean the apartment. On May 23, 1974 Mary Jane was born. It was a difficult year but we all did fine. Jane was a real trooper even though she was pregnant most of the year. We had lots of friends at the language school. Tom

Hill was the resident SBC missionary in Costa Rica at the time and he helped us out a lot. We became close friends until his death. He came and spoke at Jane's memorial service in 2010. The new language did not come easily. I walked into a coffee shop nearby and cried like a baby. I said, "You called me to go to Argentina and preach in Spanish. You will have to help me conquer this language." God told me to memorize scripture verses in Spanish like I had always done in English. I did, and when I got to Argentina and started preaching, about all I could do was quote scripture verses and ad-lib in between. We practiced some in shopping, in church on Sunday and with the maid.

After the year, we went home and had several months to pack for our life in Argentina. We packed two big crates and accompanied our things on a 30 day freighter ship from New Orleans to Argentina. The food and accommodations were good. Jane and Mary, the baby, did well and the other three kids ran all over the ship. We made an overnight stop at Rio De Janeiro, Brazil and were met and entertained by the resident missionaries there. When we arrived in Buenos Aires, Argentina, the treasurer of the Argentina Mission aided us through customs. He said the Mission would pay the sizable tip to get our things through customs. I objected because I knew how difficult it was to raise money in the churches for missions. He said, "Bob, you will soon learn the culture and customs of living in Argentina." We spent a few days in Buenos Aires before our assignment was made. I had stated that I wanted to start new churches.

The Districto Sur Baptist Church in Rosairo, the second largest city in Argentina, a church of 250 members, was committed to starting new churches. Their pastor, Samuel Libert, was one of the best pastors in the country. I was looking forward to working with him. Before we moved in to Rosario, the Mission had its summer meeting in Thea, a retreat near Cordoba. I was assigned a Jeep Estanchiera and we followed a family that had lived many years in Argentina. We made a routine stop at a guard station about halfway. I misunderstood the guard. I thought he was asking me if we were carrying any meat, "carne", but he was asking if I had a driver's license, "carnet". The other missionary helped us and we were on our way. The whole Baptist missionary family in Argentina had two meetings a year, a summer week in the mountains at Thea, and a winter week at the Seminary in Buenos Aires. They were always tons of fun and fellowship as well as tending to the business of our work in Argentina.

The mission owned a home in Rosario, so we moved right in. After two months, Pastor Libert resigned as pastor of the church to head up a big evangelistic crusade in Argentina, which was connected with the Crusade of the Americas, including all of South America, North America and Canada. The church asked me to serve as pastor. I refused, feeling I was not ready for such a responsibility. They insisted and I accepted to serve as Interim Pastor until they could call a new pastor. I served the entire four years of my term. There was a fine group of six deacons who promised to work closely with me.

There was a group of North Americans connected with an oil company living in Rosario. When they heard that there was an English speaking preacher in town, they asked if I would come and do a service in English. For four years I preached every Sunday morning an English sermon at nine o'clock while the Spanish congregation was in Bible study, and an eleven o'clock service in Spanish while the English group had Bible study. The two congregations got along well, though the Americans, even strong drinkers, did not understand the Argentines serving wine at their social events. The Argentines resented the Americans smoking in front of the church and they had to walk through a cloud of smoke to enter the Sanctuary.

BOB AND DR. ALBERTO PIZACATTI IN FRONT OF DISTRICTO SUR BAPTIST CHURCH IN ROSARIO.

We started four new churches in the four years I was there. I got a deacon to develop five studies in the Gospel of John to teach in our Wednesday night prayer service. He agreed because he knew they would be very understanding and supportive. I had four others to do the same in other books in the New Testament. After five weeks we started the first Church meeting in the Gonzales home. They would move the furniture out of their two room home and fill it with folding chairs from the church. We rotated and started four neighborhood church meetings in homes. The North Americans helped with great offerings and we developed a strong mission fund adding the pastor's salary from the budget. In one area we bought property and built a church building while the other three groups thrived as home churches.

BOB TEACHING AT THE FIRST HOME CHURCH

A group of youth and young adults would go with me in my Jeep, singing and sharing their testimonies and I would preach and give an invitation in towns of 50 to 75,000 population all over the Santa Fe Province. Many made professions of faith. We would counsel with them and give them Bibles and other materials. We visited one lady who made a strong profession of belief. She said she had always wanted a Bible. Our supply was gone so I gave her my personal Bible. I said I wish I could send a preacher or Bible teacher but we couldn't. She lived in a small hut with her husband and five children. Her sister lived in a hut just a few feet away with her husband and six children. She accepted my challenge to gather the fifteen together every morning and teach them the Gospel of John. Often we do not know the results of such endeavors. Two years later I was in the city of Santa Fe, the Capitol of the Province, to help a church that was having problems. Both families had moved to the city. She came running up to me and with great enthusiasm told me that all 15 had professed faith in Christ and were baptized members of the church.

In addition to pastoring the church, I was considered the leader of the Southern Baptist work in Rosario and the Province of Santa Fe. There were some very conservative, independent pastors in the area who did not always agree and cooperate with the convention. I was the leader of the big International evangelistic program, Crusade of the Americas, in our area. The convention had prepared very nice publicity materials for the campaign. When we voted to adopt those materials, a popular business man, lay leader in one of the churches and the area association, objected. He said we ought to print new materials. He said he had learned that it was better to change from time to time rather than use the same materials. That would cost the mission a lot of money and would not be as good. I said that there were two points of view and I quoted the Coca Cola theme, Coca Cola refresca mejor . He and the group laughed and we adopted the prepared materials.

We had lots of great experiences in Rosario. Both congregations were very active, and contributed to our main mission of building new churches. The fellowship of both congregations enriched our lives. The National Argentine Baptist Convention asked me to become head of the social work board of the convention. They have children's homes, homes for the elderly, and they wanted a greater emphasis on family life. I was just a month from leaving on furlough, so I said that I would pray about it and take some college courses to better prepare for that new ministry.

FURLOUGH TIME

1. We and another missionary couple in Argentina came home on furlough in November, 1968. It was Thanksgiving time and we stopped in Houston and spent several days with Jane's sister, Betty, and her family. Doug Watterson, a

personal friend, was pastor of the First Baptist Church in Tallahassee, Fl. He had heard that we were coming home for furlough and he offered us an apartment for the year. I went up to Florida State University to see about taking some courses to better prepare for the new ministry that the Argentine Convention had asked me to lead. The Dean talked me into enrolling in the PhD program. She said I would have a better selection of courses, more in keeping with what I wanted and needed. It was an interdisciplinary program, including psychology, sociology, and education, with a major in Marriage and Family Therapy. They offered me a job teaching marriage and family courses while I was working on the graduate program. I got my PhD in two years. They gave me credit for graduate counseling courses completed at the Seminary.

Jane taught school those two years and the kids did well, adjusting to school and being back in the USA. I was interim pastor of two churches in Tallahassee those two years. Lakeside Church called me as interim pastor. They also had an old house on their property that they assigned as a missionary residence. We lived in that home after our one year apartment ended until I graduated. When they called a pastor, I did not miss a Sunday preaching. The Fellowship Baptist Church called me as interim pastor. When that church called a pastor, the pastor at Lakeview was fired because he had an affair with someone on the church staff. They called me as interim again, and I served until I graduated. They had two great secretaries who typed my dissertation and were a great help to me.

While I was teaching the family courses, God spoke strongly to me and gave me a new calling. He convinced me that the greatest need in the world was the family life in the USA and I became a missionary to families from that time on. I was planning on returning to Argentina and assuming the position of Chairman of the Social Work Commission, but God would not turn me loose. In many ways, He confirmed that I should complete the degree and teach family courses in a University in the USA. It was not a good time for a university professor to be seeking a teaching position. The cover of Time magazine featured a university professor in full regalia pumping gasoline. I asked, "God are you sure?" Several miracles happened that confirmed His calling to me.

We had financial help with the interim pastorates, a furnished home, and Jane's teaching job. The sociology professor who was one of three on my PhD supervising committee was an atheist. He boasted openly that PINDER, a Baptist preacher, would never get a PhD under his direction. Three fellow students heard that over and over again and pledged to pray for me. I had to take three graduate courses under him. I made an A in all of them but I had to work harder than the other students. His plan was to let me complete all of the requirements for the degree and he would vote me down in my final oral dissertation defense. I took chapters of my dissertation to him monthly for his review, but I don't think he read any of them. I was weak in statistics which is so vital in research for a PhD dissertation. The professor who had been teaching statistics for all of the social sciences, left for another university. I had to take a course in the statistics department. All of the students in the class were stat majors except me. A new professor from Harvard was teaching the course. The first day, he wrote a formula on the chalk board of three walls of the room and I had no idea what he was talking about. I finished the course but I did not do well. My Dean sent me to the college of Education to take the other two stat courses required.

I did well in all of my classes and was working hard on the research to complete the degree. I knew I needed help on the statistics of my dissertation. The statistics' professors and graduate students offered help. I took a number and was assigned to a wonderful Christian professor. While working with me on the data I had collected for my study, he said he had developed a formula that really fit my data, and asked if I wanted to use it for my dissertation. I told him I was depending on him and his leadership. When the day came for my oral defense of the dissertation, my three friends were in the hall praying for me. I had received no help from anyone on my committee. The stat professor had prepared me well on how to defend. The sociology professor had never heard of the formula I was using and he could not even ask me a question. This was one of the greatest miracles that confirmed God's call.

As I was completing my studies, I searched the national collegiate journals in search of a teaching position. I was invited by six universities, all expenses paid, to apply for a position. I thought I wanted to teach in a Baptist university. I visited and was offered a position by Houston Baptist University and Union Baptist University in Memphis, Tennessee, but they both wanted me to teach everything in the social sciences. I told them my calling was clear, that God wanted me to specialize in the area of Family Studies. I signed a contract with the University of Tennessee in Martin. They really needed a PhD in the family area and offered me a higher position and salary. I had not yet visited Texas Tech and asked them to hold the contract until I made that visit.

I visited Texas Tech, they were in the process of changing deans. Both deans wanted to hire me, but the incoming dean said that he had never hired a new PhD at that salary and position that Tennessee offered. I said, I understand your position. Let me tell you my circumstances. I was a Baptist pastor, missionary to Argentina, and got my PhD with four kids. I need all of the money I can get, so I guess I will go to Tennessee. When I got back to Tallahassee, they called me and offered a compromise. If I came with the PhD completed, they would match the Martin contract. If

I came, ABD, all but dissertation, it would be a lesser position and salary. That is called motivation. The two secretaries at the church offered to type my dissertation. I wrote it in longhand and one secretary typed it. I edited it and the other secretary, who knew all the details for typing a dissertation, typed the final copy. Another miracle confirmation. We packed up and moved to Lubbock, Texas for the Fall, 1971 semester.

Chapter Seven

TEACHING AT
TEXAS TECH UNIVERSITY

I began teaching at Texas Tech University in September 1971. I had 23 of the best years of my life teaching and counseling students. With the encouragement of associate dean Maynette Williams, I jumped right in to all of the requirements necessary to become a tenured professor. Of the four professors who began teaching the same year, I was the only one to obtain tenure. You have three years to show exceptional accomplishment in teaching, research, and service to the university. If you don't make it, you are fired after three years. Later I was voted into the graduate school status and taught graduate classes. I was a popular teacher. Later I will share some of the letters and awards which I received from hundreds of students, faculty, department chairpersons, vice president and president of the university, and others outside of the university.

The department chair said that my classes brought a lot of students to our college. She asked me to teach a class across campus in the business administration building to attract business majors to take our courses. My students would recommend my class to their friends. The Dean said they still had to turn students away even though I taught multiple sections, so she asked if I would teach my marriage class in the auditorium that seats two hundred. I packed the auditorium every fall and spring the last ten years that I taught.

Enrollment in Robert Pinder's class on marriage in the School of Home Economics at Texas Tech University draws a full house every term. Pinder gives the students a few pointers on how to resolve conflicts, a serious subject that he often sprinkles with a bit of confessional humor to get the point across.

I received numerous teaching awards, letters and notes from department chair persons, Dean's, and several from the university president. The special education department asked me to develop and teach a special course on families of children with special needs, both handicapped and exceptional intelligence. My course in human sexuality was so popular that I was asked to teach it in the medical school. My undergraduate course in counseling led to the development of a field work course for our department. That course sent our students out into the city and involvement in all kinds of businesses and social agencies. We received many acknowledgements of the skills our students demonstrated. One businessman was so impressed with the students working for him that he signed up for my class as a special student. He wrote to my department chairman, the dean, and the university president about how beneficial that counseling course was to him and his business.

D/M

DESECOTTIER AND MOORE ENTERPRISES

3703 N. MESA RD.   LUBBOCK, TX 79403
(806) 747-4426

DR. PINDER,

LAST SEMESTER I HAD THE OPPORTUNITY TO TAKE YOUR CLASS FS 4331. I MUST
ADMIT, I HAD RESERVATIONS AT FIRST DUE TO THE LARGE AMOUNT OF RESEARCH AND WORK
THAT IS PART OF THE CLASS SYLLABUS. HOWEVER AS THE INFORMATION GAINED ALL CAME
TOGETHER, I REALIZED THAT ALL THE HARD WORK WOULD ACTUALLY BE OF GREAT BENEFIT.
AS A BUSINESS OWNER, WE HAVE MANY CONFRONTATIONS WITH THE PUBLIC, EMPLOYEES
AND DEALINGS WITH OTHER BUSINESS PEOPLE. DURING AN EMPLOYEE GROUP CONFRONTATION
MEETING, I HAD THE OPPORTUNITY NOT ONLY TO USE THE INFORMATION I HAD LEARNED
IN CLASS, BUT ALSO TO TEACH MY MANAGERS AND SUPERVISORS HOW TO EFFECTIVELY TALK
TO AND CONFRONT OTHER PEOPLE. THE MEETING WAS THE BEST I HAVE HAD WITH MY
EMPLOYEES IN THE THIRTEEN YEARS I HAVE BEEN IN BUSINESS. THE COMMUNICATION LEVEL
THAT WE WERE ABLE TO ACHIEVE WITHOUT HURT FEELINGS OR TOE-STEPPING WAS BETTER
THAN I HAD EVER BEEN ABLE TO ACHIEVE. I USED THE TECHNIQUES THAT I HAD LEARNED
IN INTRODUCTION TO INTERVIEW AND COUNSELING . THE PURPOSE OF THIS LETTER IS NOT
ONLY TO THANK YOU, BUT ALSO TO RECOMMEND THAT THE COURSE COULD BE MADE A PART OF
MANY MAJOR AREAS. IT WOULD BE SUPERIOR FOR BUSINESS MAJORS, RHIM MAJORS (WHO,
BELIEVE ME WILL HAVE EXTENSIVE CONTACT WITH THE PUBLIC AND THEIR SUCCESS WILL
DEPEND ON IT), AS WELL AS FAMILY STUDIES MAJORS. I HAVE RECOMMENDED IT TO MY
MANAGERS AND HAVE WRITTEN THE TECHNIQUES INTO OUR OWN PROGRAM OF TRAINING
EMPLOYEES , INTERVIEWING, DISCIPLINING AND COMMUNICATION . AGAIN, SINCERE
THANKS AND HOPEFULLY OTHER DEPARTMENTS MAY EXPAND THEIR PROGRAMS TO CONTAIN A
VERY IMPORTANT AREA, INTERVIEWING AND COUNSELING. IT IS A PART OF OUR DAILY LIVES.

CC: DEAN OF HOME ECONOMICS
    PRES., TEXAS TECH UNIVERSITY

SINCERELY,

L.R. DESECOTTIER, PRES. DESECOTTIER LEASING, IN

DS/lrd

Texas Tech University

Office of the Dean/College of Home Economics
Box 4170/Lubbock, Texas 79409-1162/PH: (806) 742-3031
FAX: (806) 742-1343

January 21, 1991

Mr. L. R. Desecottier, President
Desecottier Leasing
3703 N. Mesa Road
Lubbock, TX 79403

Dear Mr. Desecottier:

Some time ago, you wrote to Dr. Robert Pinder with a copy to me about your experiences in FS 4331. I want to thank you for taking time to write to us about your positive experiences. It is rewarding to know that the course has already been helpful to you in your business.

Thank you for sharing your experiences. Perhaps you will have an opportunity to take additional courses in the College of Home Economics.

Sincerely yours,

Elizabeth G. Haley
Dean

EGH/jw/wp2

xc: Dr. Robert Pinder ✓
     Dr. Nancy Bell
     Mary Reeves

TEXAS TECH UNIVERSITY
TEXAS TECH UNIVERSITY HEALTH SCIENCES CENTER
Office of the President

Lubbock, TX 79409-2013
(806) 742-2121
FAX (806) 742-2138

January 16, 1991

Dr. Robert H. Pinder
Associate Professor
Human Development and
  Family Studies
College of Home Economics
Mail Stop 1162
CAMPUS

Dear Dr. Pinder:

I received a copy of Mr. L. R. Desecottier's letter
to you commending you for the content and manner in
which you taught a course on interviewing and counseling, and I want to add my commendations also. Quality
teaching of the sort that brings in unsolicited letters
of appreciation is one of the most important factors in
maintaining and improving the university's reputation.
I appreciate your dedication to your teaching duties.

Best wishes for a great spring semester.

Sincerely,

Robert W. Lawless
President

Affirmative Action Institutions

I have received hundreds of letters from former students, many of them while they were still in school or recently graduated. Many of them up to thirty and forty years after graduation. In 2016 I received this letter of a contribution to the College of Human Sciences Fund for Excellence at Texas Tech University made in my honor.

TEXAS TECH UNIVERSITY SYSTEM
Institutional Advancement

October 11, 2016

Dr. Robert H. Pinder
119 Juniper Berry Trail
Georgetown, TX 78633-4706

Dear Dr. Pinder:

On behalf of Texas Tech, I am pleased to notify you of a contribution to the College of Human Sciences Fund for Excellence made in your honor. Each donation provides a unique opportunity to enrich the outstanding programs offered by Texas Tech University.

The donor information is listed below. If I can be of any assistance, please feel free to call my office at 806.834.5673.

Sincerely,

Madison Taylor
Coordinator of Stewardship Services

Donor

Mr. and Mrs. Jeffrey D. Thompson
711 East Murco Drive
Mineral Wells, TX 76067-5785

"I owe the majority of the good in my adult life- marriage, children, grandchildren – to his example and teaching. He should know that his legacy lives on in my second generation."

Box 45025 | Lubbock, Texas 79409-5025 | T 806.742.1142 | F 806.742.4037

58

When I wrote the Thompsons to thank them for their very generous donation made to the University in my honor, I received this letter.

November 27, 2016

Dearest Dr. Pinder,
I am so thrilled to write to you to give you a little of our history that you helped make possible. I've enclosed one of our Christmas cards form last year so you can see the fruit of your labor during my college years. Our children are Amber, Brandon, Chase and Danesa, and you can see all our grandchildren except for Gregory, who was born to Danesa and Zach on New Year's Day. Brandon and Corey are also expecting their first in May. So, you see, we are a family of fourteen, and you definitely played a role in strengthening our marriage in those early years. You were the very first person, whom I was convinced was a Christian, who used profanity, albeit very mild. That may seem odd to you that this was a positive thing for me, but at the time, I received your candor as a genuineness that had been missing in all the Christians" I had ever known. I was raised in a very legalistic church of Christ home, and didn't know that god loved me until I was about 30. The way you shared so openly about your relationship with Christ, even in a sometimes godless university setting, really made an impact on me. I was desperately searching for hope in a very difficult marriage, and your openness about conflict in a normal marriage was so helpful to me. I had never even considered that all

marriages had rough patches and disagreements. You helped me to see that the unhappiness I was feeling in my marriage didn't mean I had made a mistake, it was simply the melding of two personalities. Two very strong personalities, in our case! The time I spent sitting in your classes was the beginning of an ever-deepening walk with Jesus that continues happily to this day. I am thrilled to know that the new student building on the Tech campus is to be named in your honor. I cannot think of anyone who is more deserving. When you take the profound positive influence you had on my life waaaaay back in 1980 and multiply it by the thousands of students you have taught, the cumulative effect is quite staggering. May God continue to bless you with good health and great happiness every day of your life. You have always been and always will be one of the most important people in my life. I am thankful every day that God brought us together all those many years ago. Love and blessings during this Christmas season and always.

Much love,
Melinda Thompson

Two years later I received notice of a second donation the Thompsons had made to the College of Human Sciences Student Scholarship Fund in my name and a second letter from them.

TEXAS TECH UNIVERSITY SYSTEM
Institutional Advancement

September 7, 2018

Robert H. Pinder, Ph.D.
119 Juniper Berry Trail, #T
Georgetown, TX 78633-4706

Dear Dr. Pinder:

On behalf of Texas Tech, I am pleased to notify you of a contribution to the Human Sciences Alumni General Scholarships made in your honor. Each donation provides a unique opportunity to enrich the outstanding programs offered by Texas Tech University.

The donor information is provided below. If I can be of any assistance, please feel free to call our office at 806.742.1142.

Sincerely,

Wendy Wilkerson
Stewardship Coordinator

Donors

Mr. and Mrs. Jeffrey D. Thompson
711 East Murco Drive
Mineral Wells, TX 76067-5785

Box 45025 | Lubbock, Texas 79409-5025 | 806.742.1142

61

Dr. Pinder,

Since last talking to you, my husband and I have transitioned into our next chapter of life. This past May, we both walked out with our seniors and retired from public education, he with 32 years' service, and I with 22 years. We have since begun working together here at the house, as we have our entire marriage in the "off-season", and are enjoying it profoundly. Just every few days, I think of you, and what an enormous impact you and your teaching had on me as a very young, immature married person almost 40 years ago. I know for a fact that we would not still be married, let alone be so very happy together, without your influence, your personal testimony and your steady demeanor while teaching about family life. You helped me know that events which seem like the end of the world at the time are simply an opportunity to grow, to allow your spouse to "knock the rough edges off", to become more tolerant and more loving in general. In short, you were the first person who demonstrated to me that the ultimate goal of marriage is to receive your spouse as the great gift from God that he or she surely is, and to embrace your differences. In this way, we can truly move toward being the best version of who God intended for us to be. I vividly recall the day you related the story of being in a hotel room, far from home, and the song "The Cat's In The Cradle" came on the radio, and the impact the realization those lyrics brought to you about your own family. It was a very powerful moment, etched in my memory, which contributed to my subsequent parenting decisions. We happily and busily raised four active children, who have now blessed us with five spectacular grand-children. We've had challenges, as every family does, but the strong, godly foundation you helped lay so many years ago has weathered every storm, and today I can honestly say I am much more in love with my husband that at any other time in our lives, and we are so very happy in our new careers. We spend every waking moment together, most days, working and learning together, and we are just supremely blessed. Thank you so much for your part in our family and all that has come from our lives together.

I am so excited for the dedication of the new building in your honor! What a perfect way to stamp a blessing on all who will enter those doors. And how exciting for you to be interviewed by max Lucado. He is one of my favorite authors as well, and I hope to be able to read the result of your inter-view in some future story. I am profoundly grateful to God that you are well and still blessing people, and I thank God always that He put you in my life at a time when I so needed your influence. May the goodness and the grace of God cover and keep you and my you prosper in every way until Jesus returns.

Much love,
Melinda Thompson

I shared these letters with my friend Max Lucado. I recently visited with Max and I asked him to share with me his growth in God's Grace. His response is amplified in this conversation recorded on his web site.

Lucado: "I think I can say I have changed my position. I think when I was a missionary in Brazil, I came to a better understanding of grace that I didn't have before I went to Brazil. There was some latent legalism in me — and there probably still is — that I found when I was in Brazil. When we were in Brazil, our little church wouldn't grow. We thought, 'Why won't it grow?' So we started studying the Gospel, and I personally found out that I was kind of overlaying the Gospel with regulations and rules. And so I repented of that, and we began teaching the Gospel. Then, the church had its own mini-revival. It was a wonderful experience for me. I can say that in my own life, I have gone through a personal discovery of grace."

Baptist Press: This is an issue that could make both sides upset — a lot of readers and a lot of people in the Churches of Christ. Have you seen that?"

Lucado: "I think people are very understanding. We've received criticism, of course. But our thinking is that we're not here to please other churches or other church leaders in other cities. As a church in San Antonio, our goal is to reach San Antonio. Our goal is to raise up 10,000 members who will pray every day for 10 people, and thereby impact 100,000 people — which is a tenth of our city. That's our dream as a church. We're about halfway there now.... I'm sure we've disappointed some people along the way. We didn't mean to, but we wouldn't do it differently."

Baptist Press: Does your church hold to a Church of Christ view of eternal security?

Lucado: "I don't. Now, this is an ongoing conversation in our church. I believe that if a person is genuinely saved they're eternally saved, and that the work of the Holy Spirit — Ephesians 1:13, 'When you believed you were sealed with the Spirit' — that sealing is effective and eternal. If a person is genuinely saved, then nobody can snatch them out of the Father's hands. That's a discovery that I have made in the last decade or so that I don't think I embraced early on. But when you discover that salvation belongs to the Lord and doesn't belong to you, that is good news.

MY PICTURE WITH MAX LUCADO AND MY DAUGHTER, JUDY COX

I was asked to speak and lead conferences to other departments in the college, to the AHEA, the Mortar Board, the student teachers association, and other groups.

The Department Chairperson wrote in my annual report, "Dr. Pinder is a popular teacher. He teaches Early Years of Marriage, Family Life Education, and Family Counseling. He has developed a format of recruiting students who have taken the course to serve as trainers during the following semester. This works well in that it enables small group supervision and enhances the skills of the trainers who are doing the supervising. I am in charge of the field work community practicum experience for the department. Students report that this class is the most valuable that they have taken preparing them to work in the community agencies and organizations. He always receives high evaluations from students in his classes. He serves on the Faculty Council, the Teaching Effectiveness Committee, he represents our college as a consultant on the Texas Academic Skills Program. He is chairman of the University Convocations Committee, working with the Vice President to select the speaker and plan the University annual commencement service. He represented the college of Human Sciences in the University Self Study that is conducted every ten years.

HDFS DEPT. CHAIRPERSON

I served as department chairman one year but gave it up because I love teaching and not being bogged down in administration. I was featured in "The Strength of a University is Found in its' Faculty". I directed a State appropriated research grant on, The Transmission of Sex Roles Relating to Household Division of Labor among Three Ethnic Groups in Lubbock, Texas.

I developed the first graduate course in family therapy. Because of some technicalities we had to call the course, Counseling in Family Problems. After several years we added faculty and developed the program. It has become one of the outstanding family therapy programs in all the nation.

The South Park Hospital in Lubbock asked me to develop a mental health therapy program in the hospital. I got it organized and developed and had several of my graduate students working in the clinic. Later I turned it over to one of my graduate students. It was a great functioning mental health program for Lubbock.

I wrote articles for several departments of the Baptist Sunday school board in Nashville Tennessee. I was invited to teach and help to restructure the family department of the board. I spent four days with their faculty teaching them the latest concepts of family theory. I spoke and led conferences every Summer at the two Assemblies the Sunday School Board had at Glorieta, New Mexico and Ridgecrest, North Carolina.

One year I was the speaker at the singles conference, hundreds of single adults from all over the country came. There were all kinds of special conferences dealing with all the problems and concerns that single adults face. In the last session the song leader led the congregation of over 1500 in singing, "something beautiful something good all my confusion God understood. All I had to offer him was brokenness and strife, but God made something beautiful out of my life." There was not a dry eye in the auditorium. That weekend was one of the most meaningful times of confession and spiritual growth I have ever experienced.

I developed and produced a television series on relationships for the television ministry at First Baptist Church, Lubbock. We ran four thirteen episode series in the program. I used other professionals in the city from time to time to make the program more interesting. I would invite couples and individuals to talk about some of the problems that individuals and families face.

Big Ed Wilkes had a popular morning radio program in Lubbock. He would have me on frequently to talk about all kinds of personal and family issues. Every Christmas by popular demand, he would invite me to discuss loss and grief because it is such a universal problem at that time of the year.

I developed a deep friendship with Jon Randles, pastor of Indiana Ave. Baptist Church in Lubbock and Russ Murphy the college minister there. They invited me frequently to preach at the church and to lead various conferences. I also developed some parenting conferences. I preached one revival campaign.

| Volume 10, Number 10 | 8315 Indiana Avenue • Lubbock, TX 79423 | March 10, 1993 |

FAMILIES IN AMERICA ARE EXPERIENCING UNPRECEDENTED ATTACK AND DISRUPTION - WE MUST FIGHT BACK AND SAVE THE CHRISTIAN HOME!

A FAMILY LIFE RENEWAL IS COMING TO IABC!

MARCH 26-28 FRIDAY-SUNDAY

DR. ROBERT PINDER OF TEXAS TECH UNIVERSITY!

A WEEKEND REVIVAL DESIGNED TO STRENGTHEN OUR HOMES!
* Getting Your Life Together (A strong self image.)
* Building Good Relationships (Parents, Friends, Spouses)
* Knowing How To Love
* The Four Covenants Of Marriage
* God Really Cares About Our Families
* How To Have Conflict

Dr. Bob Pinder is one of the best loved counselors in the southwest! His love for students and families goes back to his days as SBC pastor and missionary to Argentina! In the Family Studies area at Texas Tech, he is in a unique position to lead us and as a deacon at First Baptist Church, he understands the Christian home! You will be blessed!

"Families are the bedrock unit of the church. Jesus wants families to prosper!"

PLAN NOW TO BE PART OF THE FAMILY REVIVAL MARCH 26-28 AT INDIANA AVENUE!

Indiana Avenue Baptist Church   *Jon Randles, Pastor*

68

I was faculty sponsor for Russ Murphy and his student ministry and spoke at several rallies that they had on campus. Russ wrote this testimony.

I first met Dr. Robert Pinder while I was the University Minister at Indiana Avenue Baptist Church in Lubbock and he was a teacher at Texas Tech. Many of our students had Dr. Pinder as their professor and all of them said the best part of being with him was that he was "real." Even though he walked so close to the Lord, he still was just a man who struggled with some of the same issues we all face.

I will forever be grateful to him for our Friday morning meetings when I went to his home just to talk. I learned so much from Dr. Pinder as he helped me see that Jesus needs to be the only JOY of my life. You see, what happened was our college group had grown from nine students to over 1,400 students coming for worship and Bible study each Sunday. (Making it the largest Sunday morning college ministry in the world.) I never meant for it to happen but somehow our University Ministry started to consume me and be the driving force in my life. I had become anxious and wondered how long our success would last. Without realizing it, our ministry had become the JOY of my life instead of Jesus.

As we talked each Friday Dr. Pinder reminded me to be thankful for all the Lord had done in my life and ministry, but to always choose to make Jesus my #1 priority. Each time we met I felt a tremendous burden being lifted off of me knowing that no matter what happened, if I chose Jesus to be my JOY, my best days were ahead.

I only have 4 earthly spiritual heroes, my grandad, J. Nolan Murphy, Welby Smith, an older friend who is like a father to me. Jim Smith, Saralyn's (my first wife of 40 years who suddenly and unexpectedly died three years ago) grandfather, and Dr. Bob Pinder. The Lord has used these three older brothers to show me what it truly means to be a Godly man. How I thank God for these amazing men of God.

Jon Randles was a wonderful pastor and friend. God richly blessed his ministry even in his illness. He passed on to heaven much too young, long before I thought of writing this book. If he was still alive he would be featured in my story. All I had was this email of our friendship and ministry together.

INDIANA AVENUE
BAPTIST CHURCH

Jon Randles
Pastor

Dec. 3, 1992

Bob –

Thank you for your encouragement and professional help. I've needed to come for some time and I'm glad the barrier is down. I truly believe it is going to help me in perspectives that will be "long term" advantageous as well as necessary to immediate emotional health.

You are a tool of our Lord.

In Christ –

8315 Indiana Avenue • Lubbock, Texas 79423 • (806) 797-9704

JON RANDLES EVANGELISTIC ASSOCIATION

REVIVALS

EVANGELISM

CHURCH GROWTH SEMINARS

DISCIPLESHIP TRAINING

YOUTH CAMPS, RETREATS, AND RALLIES

MOTIVATIONAL SPEAKING

BIBLE CONFERENCES

2313 - 19th Street
Lubbock, Texas 79401-4413
(806) 798-3113 or 797-9704
FAX 747-8928

Feb. 10, 1994

Dr. Pinder —

I was thinking of you today and stopped to pray for you and your important work. You helped me so very much at the most out of focus and self destructive period in my life. God used you!

I will never forget that and I'm grateful He continues using you!

I hope 1994 is your best year ever in the Lord's work. Thank you.

Your Friend —

J Randles

PREACHING, COUNSELING, FAMILY LIFE CONFERENCES

When I first moved to Lubbock, Dr. Jaroy Weber was pastor of First Baptist Church. He and his wife supported my ministry and attended several of the marriage enrichment seminars I led. He offered an office and asked me to do my counseling at the church. As I began to receive invitations to do Family Life Conferences in churches, he and Dr. James Dunn endorsed my ministry and we used this folder for publicity.

FEBRUARY
22 - First Baptist Church, Slaton, Texas
29 - First Christian Church, Lubbock, Texas - Marriage Enrichment Seminar

MARCH
5-7 - Oak Ridge Baptist Church, Houston Texas - Family Life Conference
14 - Second Baptist Church, College Park, Georgia
28-30 - First Baptist Church, Levelland, Texas - Family Life Conference

APRIL
2-4 - First Baptist Church, Norman, Oklahoma - Single Adult Conference
20 - Pastoral Care Institute, Snyder, Texas
24 - San Antonio, Texas - Workshop
30-May2 - First Baptist Church, Andrews, Texas - Family Life Conference

MAY
7-9 - Sugamore Hill Baptist Church - Family Retreat
14-16 - Memorial Drive Baptist Church - Houston, Texas - Family Life Conference
21-23 - First Baptist Church, Colorado City, Texas - Family Life conference

JUNE
4-6 - First Baptist Church, Duncan, Oklahoma - Family Life Conference
9-10 - Laity Lodge, Kerrville, Texas
19-25 - Glorieta Baptist Assembly to Lead Conference and speak (two
15-July 2 - weeks)

JULY
9-10 - Oak Ridge Baptist Church, Houston, Texas - Marriage Enrichment Seminar

Dr. Robert Pinder, Associate Professor of Family Studies at Texas Tech University in Lubbock, Texas is in great demand as a Seminar and retreat speaker. He has led hundreds of conferences in all areas of Marriage and Family Living throughout the Southern Baptist Convention. He has written for Southern Baptist Publications. Dr. Pinder has served as speaker and conference leader at Ridgecrest and Glorieta Baptist Assemblies. He maintains a regular schedule of Private Practice Counseling in personal, marriage, and family counseling. He is a clinical member of the American Association of Marriage and family Counselors, and other professional organizations. He is a recognized authority in areas of Personal Growth and Development, and Marriage and Family relationships. Bring your friends to participate in these conferences.

Dr. Robert Pinder is an authority on home and family life. His education for the ministry, for counseling and his Ph.D for teaching all suit him ideally for Marriage Enrichment Retreats and Family Life Conferences.

Dr. Pinder is equally at home with church groups or with secular settings in the community. He offers positive help toward more effective family living. I recommend him often.

James M. Dunn
Executive Secretary
Christian Life Commission
Baptist General Convention of Texas

* * * * *

FIRST BAPTIST CHURCH   BROADWAY AT AVENUE V   LUBBOCK, TEXAS 79401

To Whom It May Concern:

It gives me great pleasure to write a letter of commendation concerning the work of Robert Pinder. He has served in the First Baptist Church, Lubbock, Texas in Family Life Conferences, Marriage Enrichment Retreats and also personal consultations. I've found that all of his work is filled with meaningful integrity and positive leadership.

I recommend Bob Pinder to any group who is interested in this type of ministry.

Yours sincerely,

Jaroy Weber

I have preached in nearly every Baptist church in the area around Lubbock. I was interim pastor for three churches, including two years at Calvary Baptist church. I had a full-time professional counseling practice for twenty-five years in Lubbock. I had an office at various times in First Baptist Church, Calvary Baptist Church, Bacon Heights Baptist Church, my tech office and at my home. I had referrals from many of the churches in Lubbock and the area. I had several medical doctors, lawyers, business people and others to speak in my classes. They referred clients to me for counseling. I led six marriage Enrichment weekends for the First Baptist Church in Amarillo. They had a lodge at Glorieta, New Mexico with private rooms for couples. I would drive to Amarillo and ride on the bus with the group. They reserved the back row on the bus as an office for me. I would counsel individuals and couples all the way, both ways on the trip. The leader of the Young Adult department in the church was president of a bank in Amarillo. They had an extension on Bell street with a wing they were not using. He asked me to drive to Amarillo every weekend. His wife would set up appointments for counseling with 10 to 12 couples every weekend. It was a hard day but so rewarding. Many marriages were saved and others found greater happiness and fulfillment.

I led weekend family life conferences in churches all over the nation, from Florida to Pennsylvania, especially Texas, Oklahoma, Louisiana, and New Mexico. One year I travelled forty-two weekends. God really blessed these weekends. They were like revivals. I BELIEVE THE GREATEST NEED IN ALL CHURCHES, IN FACT, THE GREATEST NEED IN AMERICA IS MARRIAGE AND FAMILY LIFE.

I will never forget the weekend at the First Baptist Church in Spartanburg, South Carolina. I did not know the pastor, Dr. Alastair Walker, but their Educational Director, George Schrieffer and I were in college together. I talked with the pastor last week and confirmed the experience. I would begin on Friday night with a summary of what is happening to families today, sharing experiences from counseling. We had a breakfast for men only on Saturday morning. I have had a strong ministry with men. I feel that they are the key to a happy spiritual family. When they get turned on to family, it can revitalize a home. This church was accustomed to having a men's breakfast every time they had a revival or something similar. We had 700 men to show up for breakfast that Saturday. Their hearts and lives were really touched as I encouraged them to take the lead in their family life. It would be easy to put a guilt trip on men, but I avoided that. They went home enthused and encouraged their wives to attend the women's session. Of course the women really got involved. Saturday night we had a mini marriage enrichment time. The marriage is the basis of the family. Sunday morning we had a two hour service, combining the Sunday school hour and the regular worship time. I preached on the theme," God really does care about your family." When the invitation was given over half of the congregation were down at the altar committing their lives, their marriages, their families to the Lord. It was a spectacular spiritual experience. I saw similar experiences in churches small and large.

On three occasions, I seriously considered leaving the university and traveling as a marriage and family evangelist, but God said no, your ministry is where you are. Dr. Lowrie wrote a letter encouraging churches to receive my ministry to families.

FIRST BAPTIST CHURCH
2201 BROADWAY
LUBBOCK, TEXAS 79401
(806) 747-0281

Dr. D. L. Lowrie, Pastor

February 9, 1994

To Whom It May Concern:

Bob and Jane Pinder have been active participants in the life of the First Baptist Church in Lubbock for a number of years. During these years Dr. Pinder has been on the faculty of Texas Tech University. He has been a Christian influence on the campus as well as in the community.

During these years he has conducted marriage enrichment retreats, family life conferences, family revivals in churches through out the Southern Baptist Convention. He has been a pastor as well as a missionary for Southern Baptists in Argentina.

His area of expertise is in the family. He has been used as counselor to assist many families through times of crises. As he comes to this period in his life, he is open to God's leadership. He is ready to be used beyond the Texas Tech Campus and beyond the First Baptist Church, Lubbock, into what ever field of service God might lead. I would commend him to you if you are looking for someone who can enrich the families of your congregation, and can assist you in building a healthy church.

Sincerely yours,

D. L. Lowrie

DLL/db

Dr. Lowrie even wrote a letter for me to begin such a new m

I was very active in the churches in Lubbock. I preached in nearly every Baptist Church in Lubbock and surrounding area. I held three long term interim pastorates. When we arrived in Lubbock and bought a home, we joined the Oakwood Baptist Church just across the street. Stan Blevins, the pastor and I developed a friendship and I taught a large men's Bible class. Later I developed a friendship with Hardy Clemons, pastor of the Second Baptist church and we joined there. Judy made connections there and it became her church home until she left Lubbock.

Calvary Baptist Church called me as interim pastor and I served there and had my counseling office there for over two years. Rob got very active there. He sang with a special musical group, where he met his wife, and it became his home church until he left Lubbock. Hank Scott, pastor of Bacon Heights Baptist Church, asked me to move my counseling practice to his church. Jane and I became leaders of the single adult department. Mary was very active in the youth program. Later she heard that First Baptist Church had a strong youth program and when she decided to move, we joined her there. FBC became our church home for the remainder of our time in Lubbock.

FBC was a traditional church. I organized and taught the first couples class in the history of the church. It became a large, active fellowship, and continues to this day. Whenever we drive through Lubbock on the way to Ruidoso, New Mexico, our favorite vacation resort, a large group of the class will meet us at Buns over Texas, a popular hamburger restaurant, for an evening of fellowship. Glenna Lane, a good friend, always invites us to spend the night and that breaks up the long trip. She and her husband were longtime friends. They introduced us to lots of friends and showed us around Ruidoso and the area.

I was faculty advisor for five Christian organizations on campus, First Baptist, Indiana Avenue, Baptist Student Union, Methodist Student Fellowship, and Quaker Avenue Baptist Church. I organized a faculty Christian Fellowship and Bible study. I counseled students in my office nearly every day.

When we joined the First Baptist Church in Lubbock, we developed a great friendship with the pastor, Dr. D.L. Lowrie.

He was always supportive of me and my ministry.

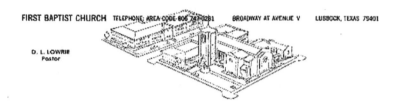

Dr. Robert Pinder and his family are active members of the First Baptist Church in Lubbock. As a husband and father, he seeks to give the positive leadership at home that he recommends to others. He has proven to be an effective family minister through marriage enrichment retreats, family life conferences and personal counselling. I would recommend him to anyone who is seeking a leader for this type of ministry. You will find him to be a man with a rich background and thorough preparation to be used of God in helping families.

Sincerely yours,

D. L. Lowrie

D.L. was elected Executive Secretary of the Tennessee Baptist Convention. FBC called Hayes Wicker as pastor. Hayes was a good preacher and had a good ministry at FBC, a traditional church. He and I were good friends. He too, supported me and my ministry and wrote this letter.

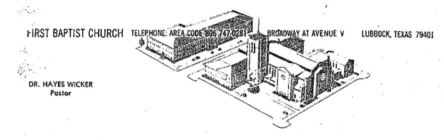

FIRST BAPTIST CHURCH   TELEPHONE: AREA CODE 806-747-0281   BROADWAY AT AVENUE V   LUBBOCK, TEXAS 79401

DR. HAYES WICKER
Pastor

There has never been a day when the home has been under
greater attack. For these difficult times God has given
servants to His people "to equip the saints for the work
of the ministry." Such a man is Bob Pinder.

I whole-heartedly recommend this faithful servant of
the Lord to minister to families and rebuild lives.
He has led marriage enrichment retreats, family life
conferences, and revival meetings in churches throughout
the Southern Baptist Convention for twenty years. He
has served as a Southern Baptist pastor and missionary
to Argentina. As a professor in the area of family,
he has faithfully ministered on the campus of Texas
Tech University for seventeen years. He has truly
been the salt of the earth and light in the darkness.

Dr. Pinder has also spoken at conferences at Glorieta
and Ridgecrest Assemblies. He has effectively taught
the Sunday School classes at the First Baptist church,
Lubbock, for nine years and has served as a deacon for
seven years. He is a churchman who knows and loves
God's people.

Dr. Pinder has a strong family which includes four
married children and four grandchildren. He practices
what he preaches and lives what he believes.

He has a great sense of humor, a pleasing speaking
voice and an attractive appearance. People can listen
to him for hours as he shares how to practically make
the family work as God intended it to be. As Soloman
said, "By wisdom a house is built and by understanding
it is established. By knowledge the rooms are filled
with all precious and pleasant riches." Proverbs 24:3-4

I trust that you will consider using this wise minister
and teacher who knows how to build our homes through
Biblical understanding and practical knowledge.

                    Dr. Hayes Wicker,
                    Pastor
                    First Baptist Church

After some years, some problems developed in the church. We lost members to Indiana Avenue Baptist Church and other churches. There was a conflict over finances between the Finance committee and the deacons, and other concerns. At one deacon's meeting it was so bad, as the chairman was about to close the meeting, I asked to speak. I said, our church is sick. I made a motion that we pray seriously for the next month and at the next monthly Deacon meeting we dispense with all regular business and deal only with the spiritual life of the church. It was unanimous. During that month, I received numerous letters and phone calls. Before the next meeting, I studied all of the materials and developed a list of eighteen major concerns. At the next monthly meeting, there were a few comments by several deacons and the chairman called on me. I began reading the list of concerns that I had developed. Hayes was in the room but did not contest anything I said. In two weeks Hayes resigned the church and accepted the call of the FBC in Naples, Florida.

The church was so divided we could not agree on a pastor search committee. We found out that D. L. might consider returning to FBC Lubbock. The Deacon body decided to serve as the pastor search committee and ask D.L. to consider returning as pastor. Dr. Lowery was so loved and respected by the church that the church unanimously called him as pastor. Under his leadership, the church fellowship was restored and grew.

This experience was positive for Hayes Wicker and for First Baptist Church. Hayes led the FBC Naples to fabulous growth and a blessed spirit. He has been one of the outstanding leaders in the Florida Baptist Convention. I recently renewed my personal friendship with Hayes. I told him about writing my life story and he sent me this letter.

First Baptist Church

3000 Orange Blossom Dr
Naples, FL 34109
(239) 597-6057

All Christ-followers should strive for "a long obedience in the same direction," as Eugene Peterson calls it. It is my joy to have pastored Baptist churches for 48 years, including the First Baptist Church of Lubbock, Texas, where I was blessed to know Dr. Robert Pinder. He loves the Lord and has served in many capacities in Christ's kingdom as a true churchman. Not many people can be described as such. He has been loyal to his many pastors over the years and served faithfully wherever needed.

Bob has been honored by the Baptist General Convention of Texas for his work as a role model, scholar, missionary and friend of students. His impact goes far beyond Texas Tech University and west Texas. He has always been heart-deep in missions, whether serving in Argentina or being a catalyst in the local church for greater mission involvement.

Countless students have been inspired by his example and character. A woman, who was a part of our university Tech ministry when I was her pastor, still fondly remembers him as her major professor. I was delighted to be reacquainted with her recently, while at the same time I was encouraged by an email from Dr. Pinder concerning my preaching and ministry.

81

A godly mentor during my days at Southwestern Baptist Seminary and in the years beyond once told me that he prayed that I would be "noble." Still winsome and joyful in his ninetieth decade, that is certainly true of Bob Pinder.

Hayes Wicker

ACTIVE IN TOTAL CAMPUS LIFE

I was active in the campus life at Tech, especially the religious life and organizations. Jess Stiles, the Asst. Athletic Director at Tech was one of my best friends. Jane and I visited regularly with him and his wife, Treva. Jess and I had lunch together frequently at the Shrimp Galley, his favorite restaurant in Lubbock. I also ate with him frequently as his guest in the Athletic dining room. I knew a lot of the athletes. The coaches and staff called on me often to help in recruiting. I met with prospective athletes and their parents to help make them comfortable with the campus and to answer their academic questions.

Spike Dykes was the head football coach at Tech at that time. He and I became good friends. He used me frequently in recruiting. This is one of the many letters he wrote to me. Bill Talley was also supportive.

TEXAS TECH UNIVERSITY

DEPARTMENT OF INTERCOLLEGIATE ATHLETICS
POST OFFICE BOX 4199 • LUBBOCK, TEXAS 79409

806 • 742-3355

February 14, 1989

Dr. Bob Pinder
Human Development
Mail Stop 1162
CAMPUS

Dear Bob,

Ten million thanks to you for your great endeavors during our past recruiting season. Needless to say how much we appreciate you taking the time with your busy schedule to help us in recruiting our prospective student/athletes.

Comment after comment have been made, not only by the student/athlete, but by their families about the indepth process that takes place on their weekend visits to Texas Tech. Certainly you would be impressed with the consideration and the enthusiastic manner in which it is done.

We would like to invite you to a very informal dinner on Saturday, March 4th in the Press Box at 5:30 p.m. to be our guest at a little ole West Texas cookout. Hopefully you and your mate can attend. Just R.S.V.P. to Patty Hargrove at 742-3355 by March 1st.

Hope you can make it and again thanks for your tremendous loyalty to this university.

Sincerely,

Spike Dykes
Head Football Coach

SD:ph

Texas Tech University
DEPARTMENT OF INTERCOLLEGIATE ATHLETICS
P.O. BOX 4199. LUBBOCK, TEXAS 79409

Memo from

BILL TALLEY
ACADEMIC COUNSELOR

PHONE 806/742-5193

December 18, 1975

Dear Dr. Pinder:

Thank you very much for your aid in helping us recruit future Red Raiders. Merry Christmas and a Happy New Year to you and your family.

Sincerely,

Bill Talley

Bill Talley

I was president of a large Dinner club in Lubbock, over 600 members. We had a monthly speaker from the National Dinner Speakers Association. At one meeting the speaker from Alaska had a wonderful program of his photography of Alaska. Some of the group asked me to plan a cruise to Alaska. We had eighteen couples join the group. Many of them were from our church and we planned to have a worship service on Sunday. I got a commitment to use the main auditorium on Sunday morning. We planned a few testimonies, someone made up a song book and I preached. We began the cruise on Saturday night. When I checked with the Cruise Director I was told he was too busy finalizing his evening show, so I left him a note. He responded that some business group had reserved the auditorium for Sunday morning and we would have the library. I sent him a copy of the reservation I had and he sent a note that we would have the auditorium. I sent him a note that I did not have cabin numbers to announce it to our group. He said he would announce it over the PA Sunday morning. He did, four times, and when we arrived Sunday morning the auditorium was packed. I announced that we did not have a song leader and a Minister of Music from Alabama volunteered to lead the singing and sing a solo. After I preached, two from our crowd gave their testimonies. Then people all over shared testimonies and we had to cut it off at noon. All week I was greeted as Pastor Pinder.

CRUISE DIRECTOR NOTE

PRINCESS CRUISES

From The Desk of Cruise Director Peter Coleman

27 MAY

TO: DR PINDER   11·30 PM.
A192

DEAR BOB,
    I AM SORRY FOR THE DELAYED RESPONSE
CONCERNING YOUR RELIGEOUS SERVICE... IT
HAS BEEN A RATHER BUSY DAY!
    AFTER INVESTIGATING, I REALISE THAT IN
FACT PRINCESS LOS ANGELES DID NOTIFY US
OF YOUR REQUIREMENTS - HOWEVER THEY
SPECIFIED THE PRINCESS THEATRE FROM 11am
UNTIL NOON. AS YOU CAN SEE FROM THE
PRINCESS PATTER, A LECTURE ON WHALES IS
SCHEDULED FROM 10am UNTIL 10·50am.
UNFORTUNATELY A MUSICIAN WAS NOT SPECIFIED
AND IT WILL NOT BE POSSIBLE TO PROVIDE
MUSIC - SORRY ABOUT THAT.
    I WILL ANNOUNCE AN OPEN INVITATION
OVER THE P.A. SYSTEM FOR 11am.

PTO →

PLEASE DO NOT HESITATE TO CONTACT ME IN THE MORNING VIA THE PURSERS DESK ON #3000 IF YOU REQUIRE ANYTHING FURTHER.

I THANK YOU FOR THE OPEN INVITATION OFFERING WORSHIP FOR ALL OF OUR PASSENGERS, A COMFORTING PROVISION THAT IS SADLY LACKING IN OUR SHIPBOARD SERVICES,

REGARDS

Peter Coleman,

CRUISE DIRECTOR.

I was a speaker several years in the Associational Farm Family Weekend celebrated in the churches of West Texas.

DIRECTOR OF A HOSPITAL CHRISTIAN THERAPY PROGRAM

Perhaps the most effective program away from the Tech campus that I was involved in was the development of the Christian Therapy program in the Southpark Hospital in Lubbock.

Dr. Frederick L. Gross, Founder and Director of the Christian Therapy Program in Palmdale Hospital Medical Center in Palmdale, California, asked me to work with him in opening and directing a similar facility in Lubbock, Texas. We met with the Southpark Hospital admin-istrators and developed the program. It was a good, very effective program, designed to meet the needs of the patient in times of acute emotional and mental stress. It is a total -person approach in which the spiritual, along with the psychological and medical aspects are used.

Dr. Fred Gross wrote an enthusiastic letter, welcoming me to the new position at the hospital.

Dr. Fred Gross

15767 LIVE OAK SPRINGS CYN. RD.
CANYON COUNTRY. CALIFORNIA 91351

February 24, 1986

Dr. Robert Pinder
Texas Tech. University
College of Home Economics
Department of Human Development
  and Family Studies
Box 4170
Lubbock, Texas 79409

Dear Bob:

It certainly was a pleasure meeting with you last week in Lubbock. I feel fortunate to have a person of your spiritual quality and commitment leading our clinical team in Southpark Hospital.

Your title will be Clinical Director and psychologist of the Christian Therapy Program, Southpark Hospital. As such you will be responsible for the overall direction of the program as well as the supervision and coordination of the clinical team and hospital staff. As psychologist, you will see patients in individual psychotherapy on a daily basis and be able to see 3 - 5 persons easily enough on a half-time basis.

Initially, (starting March 1) you will be half time, and as the program expands in and beyond Lubbock we hope your personal participation will also. We initially expect approximately 100 hours per month to be given to the C.T.P. and compensation to be $25.00 per hour. As an independent contractor, you will be responsible for any necessary insurance as well as payroll tax deposits as the taxes will not be deducted from your salary. Additional involvement on your part may include community good will and church-associated workshops, training and seminars.

Dr. Richard Beadleston on behalf of the hospital administration, wrote a warm welcome as I instituted the program and began receiving patients.

SUMMIT HEALTH Ltd.
Hospital Group
1800 Avenue of the Stars, Los Angeles, California 90067-4214
(213) 201-4000 • Telex 664224 Summit Health

Writer's Direct Line

February 24, 1986

Robert Pinder, Ph.D.
c/o Department of Home Economics
Texas Tech University
Lubbock, Texas

Dear Robert:

I wish to express my great pleasure that you have accepted the position of Clinical Director for Dr. Gross' Christian Therapy Program at Summit's South Park Hospital.

On behalf of Mr. Benton, Executive Director of South Park, and the rest of the Summit organization, I wish to state our desire for a long-term association in which pride and profitability are the rule. I am sure that having a person of your high caliber in leadership will help ensure our successful outcome.

Please contact me should I be of any help whatsoever.

Again, welcome aboard.

Sincerely,

SUMMIT HEALTH LTD.

Richard Beadleston

Richard Beadleston
Vice President, Behavioral Health Services

RB/hky

cc: Lowell Benton

Chapter Eight

RETIREMENT

I retired from teaching at Texas Tech University in June, 1994. I was still involved in counseling, the Lubbock Dinner club, doing Family Life Conferences in churches, and managing my rental property. We moved to Sun City, near Georgetown, Texas on June 7th (our wedding anniversary) in 1997. I was ready for a change and I started playing golf and tennis almost every day. The first Sunday we went to the First Baptist Church in Georgetown and joined. Pastor Jim Haskell welcomed us warmly. He had received word that we were coming from some contacts he had in Lubbock. He wrote this testimony for my book.

> *It has been my great privilege to know and work with Dr. Bob Pinder since 1997. The first time I heard the names Bob and Jane Pinder was one Sunday morning from Jack and Jeanie Simpson after they had returned from a trip to Lubbock. They said that the Pinders were moving to Sun City and that they were hard workers and great leaders in FBC Lubbock. I felt especially connected since FBC Lubbock was where my Seminary mentor was Pastor and I had been involved in paving the way for Sun City's establishment just west of the city. It*

wasn't long before this wonderful missionary/academic couple made their way to FBC Georgetown. From 1997 until my last day at the church in 2006 I can honestly say that Bob Pinder did everything he could to help me accomplish what I sensed God was leading me to do. Now don't get me wrong, we didn't always agree and hang out together but I never felt that Bob ever had anything but the best for the church and me in his mind and intentions. He was after all raised in Miami and spent many years in West Texas, two places known for sand and where you are taught to say what's on your mind. And of course he always had Jane to keep him balanced. And talk about grit...she was the first person I ever met who had both knees replaced at the same time. Bob soon moved into leadership roles in our church as it expanded rapidly. The quality of leadership that became available to us as people of tremendous experience and ability moved to Georgetown from the major population centers and mega-churches of Texas was strategic in the unprecedented growth we experienced. I am thankful I had enough wisdom to use these amazing people and that they were available and willing.

Bob helped begin a Bible Study class that became the largest class in the church and helped anchor our older adults as the church exploded with young families. He served as Personnel Chair during the greatest potential crisis I faced at the church and through his godly leadership of me and support for my decisions, we were able to come out of it stronger than we were before and tripled in growth over the number of people who left the church. One very strategic decision Bob made in particular quelled the uprising and peace soon occurred. He also taught and preached for me on many occasions and always had something important to say.

Bob also became a leader in the Baptist General Convention of Texas by serving as one of the initial board members of the Texas Mission Foundation Board and also helping to build a new BCM center at his beloved Texas Tech. One of his crowning achievements was the year his three academic loves all beat my beloved Georgia Tech Yellow Jackets. FSU beat us in Football, Texas Tech beat us in Basketball and Stetson beat us in baseball. Of all the things Dr. Bob Pinder had accomplished, that impressed me the most....just kidding!

Dr. James Haskell

Bob Ed Shotwell was Educational Director at the church and asked me to start a new adult Sunday School class. He said the only way we can grow as a church is to reach more adults and the best way to do that is to start more classes. I was serving by his direction as Director of the adult department where Jim Kramer was teaching. I asked Larry and Roene Lettow to join me and a few others followed in forming a new class. It was mostly a couples class and soon became the largest adult class in the church. Through the years it became mostly a widows class. Everybody called it the Pinder class and I did not like that. For weeks I asked the class for suggestions to rename the class. Finally I suggested the Joy class, Jesus first, others second, and yourself last. They adopted that and it is still a very active class in the church today.

LARRY LETTOW WROTE THIS TESTIMONY
FOR MY BOOK

A TRIBUTE TO DR. BOB

As a follower of Jesus Christ, we make choices every day all day long. To that end I made choices that led my wife and I to have our lives intersect with Dr. Bob and Jane Pinder's life. Following is how that happened.

My career of 42 years in the missile and space industry ended by choice, while working at the Johnson Space Center. We had lived our adult lives in California, Florida and Texas and had family in California, so that is where we thought we would retire. However, for reasons that we didn't know at the time, we couldn't go back to California.

I wanted to live on a golf course and play golf in my retirement, another choice. We didn't want to stay in Houston, so where do we go, another choice. We finally decided to go to the Texas Hill Country and that led us to Georgetown. We found a home on the 12th fairway at the Berry Creek Country Club. God is good! As was our habit, we needed to find a local church to worship at and that led us to the First Baptist Church in Georgetown.

After attending the Jim Kramer bible class for a few months, the Bible Study Director ask me if I was interested in team teaching with Dr. Bob for an adult class. I considered this opportunity and agreed to do it. The Lord blessed our teaching and our class from a few to some 50-60 people.

Working with Dr. Bob, a real man of God, was a very good experience. We became very good friends and got to know each other very much. His kindness and humble spirit exemplifies the spirit of Christ. The class members decided to name the class, JOY. Through Dr. Bob's leadership, our class enjoyed a great time of bible study and fellowship together.

We had many class gatherings together at various couples' homes. I remember a couple that took place at Charles Gates and Don Gerlinger's homes. There many more but time causes me to forget them. These were memorable because of the settings and good times that we all had.

Dr. Bob's knowledge of the scriptures and wisdom gained over the years truly was a blessing to all of us in the class. We became very close to Bob and Jane and were in their home in Sun City on several occasions. They made you feel so welcome. It is now nearly twenty years since we became friends with Dr. Bob and we have moved on in our lives, but every time we are in Georgetown we try to see Dr. Bob because of the pleasant memories that we have for him. Again by choice, we had to leave Georgetown to take care of my mother, but the Pinders will be forever be one of our close friends this side of heaven. Whenever we go to Georgetown First Baptist, we try to visit the Joy

*class and renew the friendships with those that were
there when we were.*

*Thank you Dr. Bob for the memories that you have
blessed Roene and I with over the years.*

I was an active deacon for over 20 years in the church. I
preached from time to time, Sunday morning, Sunday evening and
Wednesday night. I was active in all of the activities of the church.
I especially enjoyed the mission trips to Acuna Mexico. Charlotte
Watson, Missions Director for the church, did a great job organizing
and leading those trips. She wrote this testimony for my book.

*Since Bob Pinder and his wife, Jane, moved to
Georgetown twenty years ago, I have seen a man
who loves his Lord and loves people. Although he
had served as a missionary in Argentina for eight
years with the International Mission Board, had
pastored seventeen years in Florida, and was a professor for twenty three years at Texas Tech, none of
these are the reasons I have a great deal of respect
for Bob Pinder. That all happened in his "other life."
His new life of active retirement began when he
moved to Georgetown. He got involved immediately
at First Baptist Church when he began teaching
an adult Bible study class. They loved his teaching
plus the many ways he and Jane loved on the members of that class. My closest association with Bob
was when he went with us to Acuna, Mexico, on our
church's mission trip. His fluency in Spanish was
invaluable. Bob has been an example to all who
know him that serving the Lord continues as long*

*as God gives one breath. Even though health rea-
sons have caused him to slow down just a little, he
continues to show and share Christ at every opportunity. He is a valued friend.*

Charlotte Watson, Minister of Missions

I developed a close friendship with Associate Pastor David
Griffin who had many responsibilities in the church. I encouraged
him to get further training and put an emphasis on counseling and
working with families. He wanted me to direct his counseling
practicum but I had cancelled my certification. He took my encouragement, got his doctorate in counseling and has had a dynamic
ministry in the church. He shared this testimony.

*I met Bob Pinder when he came to First Baptist
Georgetown in 1997. I was serving the church as
an associate pastor. When I found out Bob had been
the head of the counseling program at Texas Tech,
I told him I was working on a master's degree in
counseling through a distance education program.
He immediately took an interest in me and my educational pursuits, and we developed a relationship based on our mutual interest in counseling. I
eventually shared with him that I had decided the
program was not a good fit for me and that I was
considering other options. He immediately told me
I should be working on a doctoral degree since I
already had one master's degree. I was shocked
by his statement. I had never considered doctoral
work an option because I viewed myself as inca-
pable. I dismissed his suggestion until two other
people independently told me the same thing.*

Eventually, through conversations with Bob and the work of the Holy Spirit in my life, I gained the confidence that the Lord would enable me to complete a doctoral degree in counseling. In 2007 I graduated from Denver Seminary with a Doctor of Ministry in Marriage and Family Counseling. I am so grateful for the personal growth and increased ministry effectiveness that resulted from the process of working on this degree. I am also grateful for how the Lord used Bob to encourage me, not only to start the degree, but also throughout the entire process. There were many times when I felt like giving up, but Bob encouraged me to stay the course. Thank you, Bob! It would not have happened without your encouragement.

Blessings on you!
David Griffin, Associate Pastor

Jane and I became good friends with Ed and Sylvia Rogers. When I turned the Joy class over to a younger couple, we joined Ed's class. We had a lot of fellowship with them. We invited them to join us on four of our vacation trips. Jane made sure that Ed always had plenty of coffee. Ed shares this testimony.

MY FRIENDSHIP WITH BOB PINDER

I first heard of Bob Pinder when I was a pastor in the Texas panhandle where he was well known as a Texas Tech University professor who also led in Marriage Enrichment and Family Life conferences all across the area. However, I did not get to know him personally until we joined the First

96

Baptist Church of Georgetown where he and his wife, Jane, were active members in his retirement. Bob was teaching a Sunday School class and invited us to be a part of their fellowship. That began a friendship that I have enjoyed for the last 18 years.

Years later, Bob joined the class that I was teaching and I could always count on his faithfulness as well as timely and insightful comments on the lesson of the day. We also shared a love and support of the Texas Baptist Children's Home in Round Rock.

Sylvia and I enjoyed several trips through the years with Bob and Jane as we traveled to some of their time-shares facilities. One in particular, was a week near Banf, Canada, where we together explored all the beautiful sights in the area, played many games of "42", and consumed lots of coffee. They were delightful travel companions and we were grateful they let us be a part.

Bob has been well known in Baptist circles with his heart for missions and his willingness to serve. As I have traveled through the state I have found pastors and other Christian leaders who were greatly influenced by him at Tech or in his ministry since. Bob's life stands as an example of one who keeps on serving the Lord and people even after his retirement from his vocation. ED ROGERS

Joyce said to me one day soon after we married, "Bob, you witness to everyone you meet, every waiter, store clerk, people you play golf and tennis with. Teach me how to witness." I thought the church probably has such a class. I sked our pastor, John Duncan. He said we haven't had one in the six years I have been here, why don't you teach one. As I prayed about it, God told me not to do all of the speaking myself but get the pastors and other leaders to share their experiences in witnessing. I asked Joshua Harris, the owner of Oak Ridge Ministry to alcoholics, to be the first one to share. He said I really like the approach you are taking in this class. Our group has another commitment on Wednesday nights but I am going to cancel that and bring the group here to participate in this class. They really added to the class. I called them my choir. They did not sing but stood like a military unit with a leader and in unison quoted large passages of scripture every Wednesday night. The class was so effective, the chairman of the deacons asked me to take a whole monthly meeting to instruct the deacons in witnessing.

Dr. John Duncan was pastor of FBC and married Joyce and me. We became friends and we keep in touch with him to this day. He wrote this letter for my book.

Dr. Robert "Bob" Pinder

*Novelist Walker Percy once penned poignant words, "To live in the past and future is easy. To live in the present is **like threading a needle**." I like to paraphrase Walker Percy and say, "To live in the past and future is easy. To live by faith is **like threading a needle**." The writer of Hebrews writes, "Now faith is the substance of things hoped for, the evidence of things not seen. For by it the elders obtained a good testimony" (Heb. 11:1-2, NKJV).*

When I think of Bob Pinder my heart responds in three ways: (1) gratitude for friendship; (2) a man of faith in Christ: and (3) an encourager of the saints. Bob, now in his ninetieth year, an elder, a friend, a fellow church member since I had the privilege of serving as his pastor, and a faithful follower of Christ, reminds me of a simple man of faith.

The "F" stands for "faithful." Bob has been faithful to God, his family, his church, his profession as both a pastor, and a professor, and his call to serve Christ. Every Sunday I when look up from the pulpit, Bob sits smiling in his pew, his spot in the church, in his place ready to worship, listen, and anxious to serve as a Sunday School teacher and church leader.

Let the "A" stand for "available" and "asset." Bob always stood ready and willing to serve Christ and others. His heart and commitment to Christ's church to build it up spiritually, practically, and financially speaks volumes about his character, commitment, and call in his love for Christ's people and his church. As an asset Bob raised the level of others around them through words of challenge, affirmation, and positivity.

Let the "I" stand for "increasingly." Bob lived an increasingly adventurous life, meaning of course, he still keeps moving, exploring, growing, and learning in his elder years. From Florida to Lubbock, Texas to Central Texas in Georgetown and all round the world, he increasingly seeks out and greets people with a smile. And he increasingly encourages with words. On more than one occasion his words, "John, you're doing a good job" or "Pastor, good sermon" or "Pastor, Loved your sermon this morning" sent my sermon scorecard flying high. Preachers, on any given Sunday and any given sermon, you never know, they do not always feel like they hits home runs with every sermon. Sometimes they feel they've singled or doubled or struck. Encouraging words about the sermon make the sermon feel like a homerun. And of course, God mysterious Spirit gave life in ways not always easy to record. Bob increasingly encouraged people and this preacher.

Let the T" stand for "time," "truth," and "treasure." Bob treasured time and understands the wisdom of time, life, and even hardship, the value of time in its many-faceted triumphs and travails, valleys and joys. And the treasure in time is Christ and his truth. Bob values time, treasure, and truth. Oh, and do not forget, he treasured all things Texas Tech by faith, available to watch every game and cheer his team, increasingly a TT fan, and a true Texas Tech Red Raider treasured for all time.

Let the "H" stand for "happy." Bob Pinder reveled in joy and spread happiness. I think it is because heaven is in his heart and his heart is in heaven, so to speak. By faith his life swirls with substance and with conviction and hope. After all, faith is the substance of things hoped for, the evidence of things not seen (Heb.11:1). And the substance is Christ and the hope is Christ. Bob Pinder has lived his life by faith, with the precision of threading a

100

*needle and held together by the threads of faith like
a patchwork quilt full of life, substance, hope, and
joy stitched and sewed together by Christ himself.*

*I am thankful for Bob's friendship, faithfulness, and
faith and look forward to continued friendship as
we cling to the threads of Christ.*

Love, Psalm 91, John Duncan

The Challenge of Leadership.
Being a leader is not always easy and pleasant. ,
but sometimes God's work requires you to make
decisions and take a stand that is not unanimous
and agreeable to everyone. I was chairman of
the Personnel committee at First Baptist Church,
Georgetown, Texas when the Pastor and Minister of
Music had a strong disagreement. Three times the
pastor asked me to fire the music minister. I told him
I could not do that. He was called by a vote of the
congregation and he would have to present that to
the church. He had been at the church for 20 years
and the pastor had been there 10 years. Both were
loved and appreciated by the congregation and a
church vote would split the church. The committee
worked with both men and some of their strong out-
spoken supporters for months. No compromise was
possible. Finally, the music minister found a new
ministry and retired. Although we avoided a church
split, we lost most of the choir.

Years later we faced a serious decision without a
lead pastor. Some ministerial leadership and other

church leaders proposed a major change to the Church Bylaws. Many of us felt the change violated strong Baptist beliefs and years of church practice and polity. It was discussed for weeks and hotly debated. Charles Breithaupt. Was the church moderator and explained very carefully the options involved in the decision. The church voted not to make the changes and peace was quickly restored in the congregation. Charles wrote me this letter.

From: Breithaupt, Charles cbreithaupt@uiltexas.org
Subject: Re: Proud of you, now, let's move on. Bob
Date: Jan 21, 2015, 4:10:24 PM
To: Robert Pinder pinrob@icloud.com

Dr. Bob,

Thank you for your kind words and your support! I have always valued your leadership and count you as a true Christian friend. We indeed will move forward connected in faith. But, we will not turn a blind eye to maneuvering and subversive actions. We will hold the staff and the committees to the high standards the church should expect. I have been assured that the Transition team has no intention of pushing their version of the by-laws forward. Together we will watch this carefully! I love you my good Christian brother. Let's keep our eyes and ears open. You helped save our church from what surely could have been a disaster. Let's remain steadfast in moving our church forward in a manner pleasing to God!

Dr. Charles Breithaupt
Executive Director
University Interscholastic League
Associate Vice President DDCE
University of Texas @ Austin

Chapter Nine

MISSIONS

A SUMMARY OF HOW GOD'S CALL TO MISSIONS HAS
CAPTIVATED MY WHOLE LIFE.

M issions and Evangelism has been my passion since my teenage years. It was confirmed in a dynamic call to the ministry. I was running with the wrong crowd. Six of us were stealing reflectors off the license plates of cars. The group went on to stealing bicycles and worse. God saved me and sent me back to the youth group in my church, and called me to preach. The group went on to a life of crime . Two were killed stealing radios from military airplanes. All were in jail. That is when God burned into my heart and brain that EVERYBODY NEEDS THE LORD.

When I went to Stetson University for college, I was very active in the Baptist Student Union, and all of the Christian groups and activities on campus. I preached at six jail cells at the city jail every Sunday. I had a strong Christian witness on campus. I was religion editor for the annual Hatter staff. I was religion editor for the Reporter, weekly newspaper, writing a Christian article every week. I was president of the ministerial association of over 100 preachers. I was president of the BSU on campus and the Statewide organization. I was voted one of the ten most popular students, with a full page photo in my senior year school annual. Before I pastored a church, I preached anywhere and everywhere.

My first pastorate, in my sophomore year, was Priscilla Baptist Church, a small rural church near Bell, Florida. All I knew to do was to go from farm to farm witnessing to families. That first year, the first time I baptized in my life, I baptized 18 in a cold spring feeding into the Suwannee river. Four years ago Charles, "Bo Peep" Bryant and his wife, Anita, came to Texas to visit me and brought the photo of me and the 18 in the cold spring. I did not know the photo existed. I was known as the evangelist among the preacher boys on campus. Several of them had pastorates and invited me to preach revivals in their churches. I was the preacher on the State BSU Youth Revival Team, preaching 13 revivals all over the State of Florida one Summer. I preached at Student week at Ridgecrest Baptist Assembly that year. My parents went to hear me. One afternoon dad approached me and asked me to teach him how to pray. After retirement, he became a strong Christian. He was a faithful tither and loved to pray in public.

Missions: Every day, Everywhere

Join Dr. Bob Pinder
Wednesday,
September 13,
At 6:00 p.m. in the
Fellowship Hall for
an engaging look
at missions in the
state of Texas and
around the globe!

In another chapter I share about all of the churches I pastored. I pastored a large church in Miami. The deacons and I visited prospects every week. I baptized every Sunday night for three years.

The Executive Secretary and the Evangelism chairman of the Florida Baptist Convention, asked me to start a new church in Orlando. They said Disney World and humanism is taking control of central Florida. We MUST start more churches. They bought a house in a fast growing area of Orlando. I lived in the home and began services in my living room. We built buildings and in three years we had a membership of 700.

Baker James Cauthen, the Executive Secretary of the Southern Baptist Foreign Mission Board, now called the International Mission Board, came to Orlando to preach at a statewide missions rally. I was on the platform because I had a part on the program. Jane was in the audience. Dr. Cauthen made a plea for mission volunteers. He said the spiritual needs of the world are urgent. We cannot wait for young people to heed the call, get their education and two years' experience. Why don't you young pastors who are fully prepared to go, pray this prayer. I am aware of the needs of the world. I am fully prepared to go. Unless the Lord closes the door or redirects my path, I will apply for missionary appointment.

Jane and I went home that night and talked and prayed together. strongly united, we felt we should apply. We were two years over the appointment age. A good friend, Bill Dyal, who had pastored a church near the church I pastored in Kentucky, was on the appointment staff in Richmond to review applications. In six months we had completed all requirements and were headed for the mission field in Argentina.

The mission board sent us to Costa Rica for a full year in language school to learn Spanish. It was a difficult year. Jane announced that she was pregnant. Our youngest daughter, Mary, was born just before our year ended. The older three children adjusted well to a new language and environment and schooling in two languages. Shopping and preparing meals, caring for the family, homework at night and classes all day, riding those rickety busses, was very demanding. We had a full time maid to ease the pain. I wanted so much to be able to preach in Spanish, but had difficulty learning the language. I went into a coffee finca and cried to the Lord. I know you called me. You will have to help me conquer this language. God reminded me to memorize scripture verses in Spanish as I had done in English. When we got to Argentina, my first sermons consisted of quoting memorized scriptures and adlibbing in between.

We had four fabulous years in Argentina, before coming home on furlough. God enabled me to start four new churches as I was pastor of a Spanish church and an English language congregation. There was a great group of young people who would travel with me in the jeep I drove for evangelistic rallies all over the Province. We had a speaker system and movie projector. We would set up in the Central Park of cities of 50,000 population or larger. The team would sing, share their testimony, show a short Christian film and I would preach. We had professions of faith at every service. We gave out Bibles and other Christian materials and briefly taught them what we could. I share more of our work in Argentina in another chapter.

The Argentine National Baptist Convention asked me to head their Social Work Board. They had children's homes, homes for the elderly, and wanted a strong program for families. Doug Watterson, a good friend of mine, was pastor of the First Baptist Church in Tallahassee, Florida. He heard we were coming home for furlough and offered us an apartment for the year.

I went to Florida State University to sign up for some courses to better prepare for the new assignment. The Dean persuaded me to enter the PhD program, saying there would be a better selection of courses for what I wanted. They gave me a job teaching as a graduate student to help pay expenses. God gave me a new calling. He said the greatest need in the world is families in the USA. From that time to the present, I became a missionary to families. I served as Interim Pastor of two churches in Tallahassee.

I felt a new calling, to teach Family Studies in college. It was not popular to be a professor looking for a job. The cover of Time magazine pictured a professor in full regalia pumping gasoline. I had invitations from six universities. Two Baptist Universities offered me a job but they wanted me to teach everything in the Social Sciences, and I felt strongly that I should teach only family studies. I signed a contract with the University of Tennessee at Martin. They needed a PhD so badly in the family area they offered me a higher position and a better salary.

I had not visited Texas Tech who had invited me. I signed the contract but I asked permission to visit Tech. They were changing Deans at Tech. Both Deans wanted to offer me a position but the new Dean refused to match the contract I had. I said I understand your position, but I have been a pastor, a missionary, and got my PhD with four kids. I need every nickel I can get, so I guess I will go to Tennessee. When I returned to Tallahassee, they called me with a compromise. If I came with PhD in hand, they would match the Tennessee offer. If I came ABD, all but dissertation, it would be the lesser position and salary. That is called motivation. The church I was pastoring had two great secretaries. I wrote my dissertation in longhand. One secretary typed it. I edited it and the other secretary who knew how to do the footnotes, etc., for professional documents, typed my finish copy. There were other miracles involved in completing my PhD in two years, shared in other chapters. With diploma in hand, we packed and drove to Lubbock, Texas to spend the next twenty-three years on the faculty of Texas Tech University.

I saw Lubbock and the Tech campus as my new mission field. I preached in most of the Baptist churches in the area. I made sure my students knew my commitment to Jesus Christ. They would spread the word and their friends would sign up for my courses. I had a strong Christian testimony in my classes and throughout the university, city, and west Texas. I sponsored five Christian groups on campus, and started a faculty Bible study.

In addition to a full time tenured faculty position, I had more than a full time private counseling office, and I did Family Life conferences weekends all over the nation. One year I travelled 42 weekends. Talk about missions, I had the most rewarding experiences of my life. The F.L. Conferences were like revivals in the churches.

One weekend God really visited and blessed in a Family Life Conference in Spartanburg, South Carolina. George Schrieffer, their Educational Director, and I were in college together. He heard about me leading these conferences and had the church invite me. I did not know the pastor, Dr. Alastair Walker. He told me later that he started to just turn that weekend over to George. Their church is very evangelistic and have had all of the great evangelists to lead revivals. He said that family weekend was the greatest revival the church had ever experienced. The program for the weekend goes like this. We began on Friday night with the whole church assembled, and I gave an introduction/ orientation for the weekend, dealing with some family issues, balancing problems and needs with successful programs for change and growth. I used illustrations and testimonies to set out some principles for wholeness and spiritual growth.

Saturday morning we had a breakfast for men only. I have a strong ministry with men. I feel that fathers are the key to a happy family life. We have made a big mistake in family life by implying that mothers should take care of the family while fathers go out and provide the income. Too many men, whether successful or not in providing for their families, have been absent from the family interaction and neglected their role as head of the family. It would be easy to put a guilt trip on fathers about family life, but I am very careful to avoid that. Most fathers want to be more active and effective in their family. They don't know what to do and how to begin. They need a simple specific plan and encouragement, not blame and constant criticism.

This church was accustomed to these breakfasts for men and over 700 men showed up. I tried to encourage them and praise them and give them some suggestions how to get started. Their hearts were touched. They went home and enthusiastically told their wives, you must go hear this man. The women turned out in large numbers for the special session for women.

On Saturday night I had a mini marriage Enrichment retreat and marriages were really touched. Marriage is really the key to building a happy family. A troubled marriage can destroy the whole family. That is why I enjoy leading marriage Enrichment retreats. On Sunday morning, we had a two hour service, combining the Sunday school hour and the regular worship service. I preached on the theme, "God really does care about your family." a positive picture of happy successful families, using a lot of illustrations of problems families have faced and how God and His word gave them victory and success. God so blessed and gave power to that message by His spirit. It was a summary and climax to what they had experienced all weekend. When the invitation was given, over half of the congregation were at the altar, committing their lives, marriages, and families to the Lord. I have experienced that in churches small and large all over this nation.

We were very active in the First Baptist Church, Lubbock. I started a couples Bible class that became the largest adult class in the church and continues to be very active. I began a Spanish ministry. I felt they needed a native speaking teacher. A young man committed to the ministry and I worked with him and then turned it over to him.

When we retired, Jane and I moved to Sun City, Georgetown, Texas. We immediately began Bible studies in our home. The group grew and we moved to the library in the social center. One of our friends took over the teaching and we got more active in the First Baptist Church. I was asked to start a new SS class. Jane and I were both very active in the mission activities of the church. We went on mission trips with the church group. Jane and I travelled a lot and all of our trips involved mission work. We spent two weeks every year in Puerto Vallarta and were active in the English speaking church and their mission work. I met pastor Sotomayor of the Hay Esperanza Baptist church. We became good friends. He would ask me to preach every year. We took a big supply of Bibles and tracts. The treasurer of the church nearly had a heart attack. She said we cannot afford that expense. The pastor calmed her down and told her that was a gift of the Pinders. He had a great ministry to Prostitutes in the city. He taught them to sew for a living. As I presented the prayer needs to my SS class, one lady offered a sewing machine which we gave to this ministry to prostitutes.

On one trip to the Dominican Republic, we had made contact with the administration of a mission school and we were able to minister to the students and faculty and develop a strong friendship with the administration. When we arrived, we were tired from the trip so before getting settled we went to the pool to refresh. I was sitting in my bathing suit beside the pool. Out of the blue, a young man walked directly up to me as if he knew me and I thought OK what kind of a sales pitch is this going to be. He was very friendly as if he just wanted to visit and converse. I talked with him for some time and found out a little bit about his life, family, and work. Then I began to witness to him and he was very interested. I asked him if he would pray to accept Christ, he seemed so interested, so ready. He said, I cannot do that. I could not live as a Christian at this place, look at all the drinking. I explained to him that he needed the Lord all the more in that environment and that Jesus would help him and give him strength to face whatever he had to face. He was really anxious and he said he was ready. Right there beside the pool with this preacher as his support, he prayed the sinner's prayer to receive Christ as his Savior. Sometimes we wonder how sincere and what kind of experience this really is, but we saw all week a changed young man. He had a testimony in his heart that was evident. He shared with us how he shared his new found faith with his family and also at work. We could see all week the difference that Jesus made in his life. This is Paul's message all over again when he says," I am not ashamed of the gospel of Jesus Christ for it is the power of God unto salvation to everyone who believes." Mission accomplished, I said to myself. I have had so many similar experiences. Our vacation trips became mission ventures.

One day Joyce said to me, Bob, you witness to everyone you meet under any kind of circumstance, teach me to witness. I felt that others needed to be reminded how to witness also, so I went to our pastor, Dr. John Duncan, and asked, have we had a witnessing program in our church. He said not in the six years since I've been here. Then he said, Bob, why don't you teach one. He set up a class for three hours on every Wednesday night. God told me to use leaders in the church and others who are strong Christians to share their experiences in witnessing so it would not be just Bob's experience and voice. I immediately thought of a young man who had experienced a dynamic conversion from alcoholism and drug addiction to a dynamic ministry for Jesus. He had established a ministry to alcoholics and drug attic's that was a vibrant ministry in our community. I invited him to come and share his testimony. He came the very first session that we had and brought with him two young men who have graduated from his program and were helpers in his ministry. After Joshua shared his dynamic testimony, while his associate was sharing his testimony, Joshua turned to me and said Bob I really like what you are doing here. He said the 10 men who are active in my program right now have an engagement every Wednesday night at another church but I'm going to change that program and bring them here every Wednesday night to participate in this witnessing training program. His program was not just an alcohol drug addiction program it was a strong discipline gospel program. They memorize long passages of scripture. I had them stand as a group and speak the Scriptures they had learned. One of them would be the leader and it was almost military style. The leader would call them to attention. They would stand and quote long passages of scripture from memory. I called them the choir for my witnessing class. They really inspired everyone. That witnessing class was so effective the chairman of the deacons asked me to take a whole deacon meeting to teach the deacons how to witness. Joyce became a very effective witness and will not leave the house without Christian tracts to share the gospel.

Baptist student ministry has been a central ministry in my life since college days. I worked closely with all of the BSU campus directors at Texas Tech. Bruce McGowan was a special friend. After leaving Tech he became the state wide director of all BSU ministries in the state. He wrote this letter.

Texas Baptist Convention
bruce.mcgowan@texasbaptists.org

The foundation of effectively communicating the Gospel message by campus ministries such as Baptist Student Ministry is found through Christian Faculty Sponsors! Dr. Bob Pinder before, during and after I served as the BSU Director formed that foundation not only for BSU but also a number of other evangelical campus ministries at Texas Tech. Year after year Dr. Pinder encouraged and challenged campus ministers like myself as he shared his testimony in classes, pushed students toward our ministry and was directly involved as chairman of our Baptist Associational committee. His support was way beyond what was expected and experienced with other sponsors. Often students would share how Dr. Pinder's boldness in sharing his testimony in class encouraged them to be bold, his counsel formed the basis of major life decisions such as finding a Christian spouse and helped countless students as they navigated being a Christian at a state university.

One benefit of serving as a campus minister is having your children impacted by College Students. Mary Pinder Brinkley, Dr. Pinder's daughter was involved in BSU at Texas Tech and babysat our two children. She is a reflection of the character and life of Dr. Pinder as we saw her love and serve our children.

After I left Texas Tech to serve in Texas BSM statewide I had the privilege to reconnect with Dr.

Pinder as he served faithfully on the Texas Baptist Missions Foundation giving further support for funding Texas BSU through that entity of the Baptist General Convention of Texas. To have his name on the new BSM building at Texas Tech is most fitting of a life lived for Jesus Christ impacting Dr. Pinder's family, community, work, campus community at Tech and mine personally. Thank you Dr. Pinder for blazing a trail for all of us to follow in our pursuit of Jesus.

Blessings,
Bruce McGowan, DMin. Director, Center for Collegiate Ministry

Cindy McBrayer is currently on the staff of the Texas Tech BSM. She leads a dynamic ministry with international students. She shared this letter with me.

I have fond memories of Dr. Pinder's association with the Texas Tech BSM (BSU) during my days as a college student (1971-75) and as the associate BSU director (1978-83). As I recall, he was a regular speaker at both our noon luncheons and evening programs. I knew he was a well-respected and highly sought after professor by everyone who took "Interpersonal Communication" at Texas Tech. I really wanted to take his class, even though it was not a requirement in my field of study, just because I kept hearing from my friends how good the class was, and how much they loved Dr. Pinder! Unfortunately, every one of my elective hours was spoken for, and I was not able to take the class.

One of the reasons I was so impressed with Dr. Pinder was because I knew he had served as a missionary to Argentina with the IMB, and I was extremely drawn to any and all things missional. I was so impressed with how he considered the Texas Tech campus to be a continuation of his missionary service. I carried that same attitude with me into the public school classroom, where I taught French and Spanish for twenty-nine years. However, my love for international missions never ceased, and during my seminary studies, I had the opportunity to attend a retreat for international students studying on Texas campuses. That opportunity led me to see missions in a whole new light.....and my husband and I began hosting international students in our home on a regular basis. I began praying for an opportunity to work with international students in ministry, and upon retirement (at age 59!) from my teaching career, I was blessed with the opportunity to return to the Tech BSM and serve as a Cross-Cultural Specialist, focusing on international students.

Being the "senior" staff member at the BSM has given me the advantage of being able to remember the rich relationship between the BSU/BSM and Dr. Pinder. It has been a real joy to be able to spend time with him these past few years, as he has so generously given the Tech BSM ministry the opportunity to continue ministering to students from around the world for generations to come. I have enjoyed sharing with him the stories of international students who are deciding to put their trust in Jesus, risking losing everything they know and love to do so. God opened my mind and heart to students coming from Muslim backgrounds, especially those coming from Iran. Our BSM has seen a dozen Iranian students decide to follow Jesus while studying at Tech. Their stories are so inspiring and courageous. Some of these students have truly forsaken their families to follow Jesus, just as he said in Matthew 19:29. Many are now leading other friends and family members to follow Jesus. Watching these new disciples grow in their faith has made me realize what the Christian commitment really means. It is a joy to see God working in this unexpected way (although we really SHOULD expect it)!

I know that Dr. Pinder is a man of great faith and prayer, and that he is praying for me, for the Tech BSM ministry, and for these new Christ-followers as they seek to lead their friends and families to follow Jesus, too. Once a missionary, always a missionary, and Dr. Pinder definitely still has a missionary's heart!

Cindy McBrayer

3A

I met Dr. Pinder during a family crisis. My husband had just
learned that he had terminal cancer and was not expected to live 6
months. We were told to go home and get our affairs in order. I
had never been involved in the planning of a funeral so I googled
Lubbock funeral sites. I saw an advertisement about someone
selling a plot in Lubbock. I called about it and that's when I met
Dr. Pinder. I sobbed to him about Jay and he talked to me about the
Lord and prayed with me. When it came time to transfer the title
into our names, he charged us less than the price quoted in the
advertisement. Since that time, Dr. Pinder has been consistent to
contact us and to pray for us. Jay lost his battle to cancer July 8th
and Dr. Pinder has contacted me several times since then. He was a
beautiful part of our journey. He is kind, giving, loving, loyal and
Godly. He is a true example of what a Christian should be. God led
us to Dr. Pinder and I will forever be grateful.

In Christ,
Jana Watson

Dr. Pinder - there are no
words that say thank
you enough for your kindness.
You have been a blessing to
my wife, myself & my girls.
May God Bless You
Jay Watson

For you're among
the nicest people
I have ever known,
And you'll never be forgotten
for the thoughtfulness
you've shown.

Thanks for Everything

Dr. Pinder - thank you so much again for your
kindness. Truly, I will never forget
how you have blessed us! I
love you & I pray Gods richest
blessing on you & your family.
In Christ,
Jana

Chapter Ten

OTHER MINISTRIES IN RETIREMENT

Y ou never retire from the ministry. The need is always there and if your eyes and heart are open, God will put you to work. After I retired from teaching at Texas Tech and was finishing up my tenure as President of the Lubbock Dinner Club, my rental property, and other responsibilities, we made several trips to consider moving to Sun City, Georgetown. On the third trip, Jane felt strongly that we should move. I played golf, shot a 76, and decided, this is where I want to live. We bought a home that was under construction. On our way home I thought what have I done? I have my home, three houses, and six duplexes that I have to dispense with. I asked three realtor friends about the market. They told me it was bad. There were thirteen houses for sale within two blocks of my house and no movement. I did not have enough hope to put an ad in the newspaper. I put an ad in the thrifty nickel, the grocery store free paper, for sale by owner. I used some meaningful words, creative finance. Nobody knew what it meant, neither did I, but it brought people in. Many people wanted to buy a home but did not have the money. They could not afford my home but I sold the other three homes. I found buyers for the duplexes. A couple were very interested in my home but did not have the money. He had recently moved to Lubbock and had a good job. He gave me his 401K and we made a contract for sale without transfer of deed until he could finance it at a bank. We packed up and moved to Sun City in 1996, one of the early residents.

As a Texas Tech fan, I was a stranger in a foreign land. Everything was UT, A&M and Baylor. I played golf and tennis, wearing my TT cap. Whenever I met anyone with any interest in Tech, I got their email address. I started a TT support group listed in the Sun City monthly magazine. We had a great turn out, set up a leadership structure, sent out regular emails. We had all kinds of activities, especially speakers, socials, sports events. It really grew, and became an official Texas Tech Alumni Association Chapter. The group named it, the Dr. Robert H. Pinder Chapter. When we moved, there were over 300 members.

ONE OF THE LEADERS IN THE GROUP WAS ROBERT WOODUM. He wrote this letter when I retired from the leadership of the Chapter.

Dr. Pinder,
Thank you for your diligence and vision in the work that you and Joyce did in creating the foundation of Texas Tech Alumni that lead to the Georgetown Chapter of The Texas Tech Alumni Association. We all owe you a debt of gratitude for your long term persistence in the ups and downs that go along with getting an organization started.

I will continue to do my part in helping it grow and in working alongside you, Truett and all the other Red Raiders in the future projects of the Chapter as long as I am still in Georgetown. We are all blessed to be living at this place and in this time together to enjoy the richness this area and the great fellowship that God has given us.

The Dr. Robert H. Pinder Chapter of the Texas Tech Alumni Association has a dynamic life and a great future. Dr. Pinder has been named President Emeritus.

ALL THE BEST, ROBERT WOODUM

Guns Up!!!

The Oaks Retirement home invited us to tour the home and have a free meal. We seldom turned down a free meal. They asked when do you want to come. I asked when do you serve your best meal. They said Sunday. When they found out that I was a retired pastor, they asked if I would preach on Sunday. I agreed and later they asked if I would preach every week. It developed into a regular church group with about forty-five in attendance.

The group asked to take an offering. They gave generously and we supported the NEST EMPOWERMENT CENTER of the Georgetown Project program, a strength-based program to build assets in the youth, a safe haven for high school students who are homeless, at-risk, or living in transition. The managers considered me an unpaid chaplain and really supported our ministry. The group asked for a weekday Bible study. I enlisted eighteen deacons to alternate weeks in teaching. Dr. Ed Rogers agreed to be the master teacher with an organized curriculum. When we moved, I surrendered the leadership of that ministry to that group of deacons. Also, we had deacons to come quarterly to administer communion.

BOB PREACHING AT THE OAKS RETIREMENT HOME

THE DIRECTORS REALLY SUPPORTED MY MINISTRY FROM THE BEGINNING. THEY CONSIDERED ME AS AN UNPAID CHAPLAIN. THEY ASKED ME TO LEAD THE INVOCATION PRAYER FOR THE FORMAL OPENING.

I found lots of ways to share my Christian testimony. It was a daily experience. It seemed that God presented an opportunity at every turn. I am convinced that God would spontaneously put ideas in my head and as I acted on them, He had a plan in motion.

I was very active in civic affairs in Georgetown. The Dr. Robert Pinder Chapter of the Texas Tech Alumni Association was involved in many activities. The church at the Oaks Retirement Home that I pastored was active in the Teen Program of the Georgetown Project. First Baptist Church had service projects all over town. The Mayor of Georgetown proclaimed February 3, 2018 as Dr. Robert Pinder Day in Georgetown.

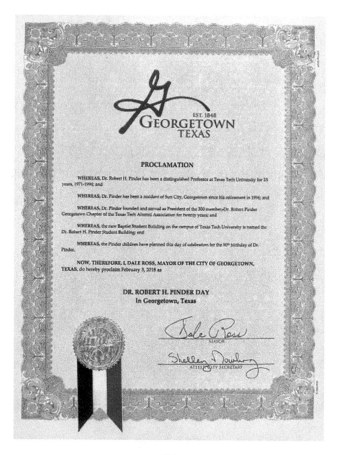

I wrote this song one early morning. I had an eight o'clock dermatology appointment. It was on my mind and I woke up early and started singing and writing this song. I wrote half of it at home and then finished it in the doctor's office. She walked in and said, what are you writing and I told her I am writing a song. She said sing it to me and so I sang it and she got all excited about it and went out and got another doctor and two nurses and brought them in and said sing it for them. You never know how God can multiply your witness. This is the song.

"You gotta walk that lonesome journey. You gotta walk it by yourself. Nobody else can walk it for you, you gotta go there all alone. But my God has made a promise, if you trust him he'll be there. It takes faith and a little practice but if you try you can make it fine. God has promised to walk it with you, bear every burden, every care. Gather up your Christian brothers they can help your problems bear. Take a walk along with Jesus. He'll be with you everywhere. And that promise you can count on, eternal life he wants to share. There's a home in heaven for you, all prepared and waiting there. Take along somebody with you and all the blessings you can share."

When Charles Wade was Executive Director of the Baptist General Convention of Texas, he wanted to do more than had ever been done for missions. He knew we needed a new, daring approach and organization to get the churches of Texas uniquely equipped and motivated to reach this world with the Gospel of Jesus. He got a group of the best missionary people in the state to form a study group that later became World Connex. He invited me to become a member of that founding group. Bill Tinsley was named to head up that organization. A great structure and plans were developed but it is hard to change years of " we always did it this way". A lot of money was invested, some unique things were accomplished, but the churches never got enthusiastically involved. Bill Tinsley wrote many notes commending me for my insights and commitment to Worldconnex.

The state of Texas owned property at Junction, Tx. For years it was given to Texas A&M and they used it for a training ground for their football team. The people wanted a school. It was transferred to Texas Tech. The Tech President and my Dean knew that my classes were popular and asked me to travel and teach my class there. The local Baptist pastor took my class and brought a lot of his congregation. It became successful and I also had a strong witness in the church and community. My son Rob went with me often and we canoed the local river and had good times together.

Texans, for Lawsuit Reform, TLR, was formed in 1994, the year I retired from teaching at Tech. It is a volunteer – led organization working to restore fairness and balance to our civil justice system through political action, legal, academic and market research, and grassroots initiatives. I worked a lot with several lawyers in Lubbock as a professional witness, etc. Two of them recommended me to the Governor and I was named a founding member of the Board of Directors of TLR. I have been elected every year since, named by each Governor. I took my attorney, my nephew, Keith Gamel to one of the Board luncheon meetings in Austin. It is a great organization for common-sense Lawsuit reforms. Here is the recent report of TLR.

FEBRUARY 2019

TLR ADVOCATE

TEXANS FOR LAWSUIT REFORM. MAKING TEXAS A BEACON FOR CIVIL JUSTICE IN AMERICA

FEBRUARY 2019

OUR MISSION

Texans for Lawsuit Reform is a volunteered organization working to restore fairness and balance to our civil justice system through political action, legal, academic and market research, and grassroots initiatives. The common goal of our more than 18,000 supporters is to make Texas the Beacon State for Civil Justice in America.

1701 Brun Street, Suite 200
Houston, Texas 77019

www.torreform.com
tlr@tortreform.com

f 🐦 @lawsuitreform

Disorder in the Courts

By Richard J. Trabulsi Jr., TLR Chairman

After more than two decades of tort reforms enacted by the Texas Legislature, it is time to give increased attention to the organization and efficiency of the Texas court system. The TLR Foundation issued a comprehensive review of the Texas courts in a 2007 paper, *Recommendations for Reform, The Texas Judicial System*. That paper generated widespread interest, leading to the establishment of a State Bar of Texas Task Force on Court Administration, which issued an October 2008 report that made many recommendations to rationalize the Texas judicial system.

The Task Force Report refers to Alexander Hamilton's Federalist No. 17: *"The ordinary administration of criminal and civil justice...contributes, more than any other circumstance, to impressing upon the minds of the people affection, esteem, and reverence toward the government."*

Our civil courts must resolve disputes between our citizens when all other avenues of dispute resolution have failed. They must give effect to the policies enacted in statutes and assure that our administrative agencies fairly and rationally enforce regulations. Our criminal courts must protect the innocent and punish the guilty. To do these things in a manner that evokes the esteem and reverence of the citizenry, our bench must be occupied by competent and impartial judges. And court administration must be organized to avoid undue delay and unnecessary expense.

Texas has 14 intermediate courts of appeals—almost three times as many as more-populous California, which has five. Texas has one more intermediate appellate court than the number of intermediate appellate courts in the federal system, which covers 50 states and the District of Columbia.

Depending on the workload of any one of our state courts of appeals, cases are transferred from one court to another, meaning a trial court judgment in, say, Fort Worth that is appealed to the Fort Worth Court of Appeals might be transferred to and decided by the El Paso Court of Appeals. The state is also divided into 11 judicial administrative regions. These regions do not coincide with the courts of appeals' districts or with district court districts. A district judge in Texas can have his decisions appealed to two different courts of appeals and be answerable to two different administrative officers.

At the trial level, we have both county courts at law and state district courts, whereas a rational system would have a unified trial bench to hear all matters of similar jurisdiction. To make matters worse, our partisan election of all judges results in periodic electoral sweeps that remove from office many experienced and highly qualified judges for no good reason.

TLR has proposals to rationalize our court system to make it more administratively efficient, to improve access to justice, and to have cases resolved in less time and with less expense. You can read about a few of those proposals in this *Advocate*.

When Joyce had her heart attack and was so weak, we joined the Worship Place, the interdenominational church in Sun City. We lived just two blocks away and the hours were very convenient. We had attended there many times and knew the pastor and many members. We got very active, especially in a large Bible class, taught by Gary Allen and Ann Hay, the wife of a former pastor.

Gary was the head of the men's ministry and had me speak to the men's group. They both called on me frequently, especially to pray. Ken and Mary Roach were greeters and Ken would have a cup of coffee prepared for me before I could sit down every Sunday. Ken sent me this note when he heard I was writing my book.

> *I first met Bob when he attended our Sunday Bible Class. It was as though he was already friends with everyone in class, even if he had never met them before, I suppose that's because he apparently has never met a stranger. Bob obviously has a lot of good traits but one stands above all the others – the way he prays! It's as though he is sincerely carrying on a conversation with God with a voice that only God could give him. I almost expect to hear trumpets playing in the background. I would love to pray like that but I don't dare because everyone would only think I was trying to be like Bob, which wouldn't be a bad thing to do. Bob and I only had a brief friendship but he will always be special to me! God bless you Bob.*
>
> *Your friend in Christ, Ken*

I have student letters throughout the book. These two letters just arrived. Randy Steele said that taking my marriage class fired him up and really encouraged him to get serious about his education. He wrote the Dean with encouraging words about my class.

Randy Scott Steele
2601 45th Street
Lubbock, Texas 79413

Dr. Elizabeth Haley
Dean, College of Home Economics
Texas Tech University

Dear Dr. Haley,

I would like to take this opportunity to share with you one of the most enjoyable experiences I have had since becoming a student at Texas Tech. I was enrolled in Dr. Robert Pinder's "Early Years of Marriage" class during the Spring of 1988. I would like for you and others to know that you are really missing alot of fun!

Dr. Pinder brings a refreshing, positve, and pro-marriage approach to the class that leaves the student with the idea that sharing your life with another person can be fun and is something to look forward to. Goodness! I actually found myself looking forward to going to class! I give my permission to share this bit of information with the entire department. I will share it with the entire university.

Dr. Pinder arrived each class day well preprared and would generally begin with a "pop" quiz. This made me prepare more thoroughly for not only his class but my other classes as well. I even began to, well, ... study. There, I said it. It only hurt a little bit. I had my best attendance record ever in his class.

I have been told numerous times during my college career the reason I must take certain courses is so that I will be a "well-rounded" person at the time of my graduation. These courses are supposed to prepare me for the "real world" in such a way that I will be able to contribute to it. My question is, why isn't a great course like Dr. Pinder's a required one? Our interpersonal relationships are critical to our own overall happiness! I am a better person because of this course. I feel a bit sorry for those who have never enrolled in it.

In closing, I offer my sincerest thanks to you, the College of Home Economics, and to Dr. Pinder. This class made my semester both memorable and enjoyable. Congratulations on a great course and to a super teacher and friend. I am looking forward to my next class with him in the Fall of 1988.

With Thanks,

Randy Scott Steele

S. I can't type so please don't laugh.

Sue Key had graduated and was working as a professional Social Worker in the Texas Department of Human Services. She wrote the Dean of the college to express how much her four years of studies had so well prepared her for her career. She focused on my counseling class as a key to bringing all of her studies together.

March 23, 1987

Dr. Elizabeth Haley
Dean, College of Home Economics
Texas Tech University
Lubbock, Texas 79409

Dear Dr. Haley:

So many times since my graduation from Texas Tech University in December, 1985, friends and co-workers have asked about my Home Economics degree which, proudly framed, dominates my office decor. "How could a background in Home and Family Life prepare you for working as a social worker with aged and disabled people?" "What good is a study of human development and counseling skills, much less studies in clothing, interior design and finance?" I am pleased to speak for the university and the College of Home Economics in answering their questions.

Economics is really nothing more than doing the best with one's resources. Daily, as I enter the homes of elderly people in Lubbock County as a representative of the Texas Department of Human Services, I am helping them to manage their energies, ideas, goods, monies and community services. Their lives are enriched in the process of redefining their resources or doing well with what they have.

The best tool that I learned in the College of Home Economics was listening with the heart. Dr. Bob Pinder's counseling class was a good developmental experience where the skill of listening was fine-tuned in a lab setting. I have come to realize that a loving listener is best prepared to facilitate a client's needs. At that point, other tools learned in Texas Tech's College of Home Economics can be employed, such as designing a wardrobe or a work space for the handicapped or say assisting the elder citizens with financial or nutritional planning. Listening with the heart is, for me, immeasurably important as a social worker who is collaborating with a client to ensure the best possible management of resources.

Perhaps it is a mistake to mention courses and professors' names specifically. It is enough to say that, without exception, the studies made inside the halls of Texas Tech University's Home Economics College have been very valuable to me professionally and privately.

Dr. Pinder has been a life changer for me! His class at Texas Tech was one of the best classes that I have ever taken. His definition of marriage as two whole complete persons hacking it out together is something that has been ingrained in my head and I ponder it often! I feel so blessed to have had him as a professor and to still be a part of his life today! He is truly one of a kind!

Tara Knight
Keller Williams Realty
512-751-4834 Direct
512-579-4219 E-Fax
512-439-3652 Office

After my missionary service in Argentina, I got my PhD and came to Texas to teach at Texas Tech. I have been very active in many churches and in retirement I served thirteen years on the board of directors of the BGCT Missions Foundation. During most of those years Dr. Charles Wade was Executive Director of the Baptist General Convention of Texas. He wrote this letter for my book.

> *I am so glad that Dr. Bob Pinder is writing his life story. He has a wonderful, exciting, God blessed life story to tell. It is a life worth knowing. You will be blessed and encouraged by this book. His life has been full of adventure in the service of God. He has been a successful pastor, missionary to Argentina, University professor, Marriage and Family Therapist, and an exceptional student worker. Thank you, Bob, for your encouragement and support through the years.*

Charles Wade

After Jane's passing, I made a special trip to Israel. I had regularly received Dr. Jim Denison's daily devotional. He announced that he was taking a group to Israel. After I made contact, he told me that he was taking a large group from Lubbock. I knew all of that group. I had counseled with three couples. Later I discovered that the sponsors for the tour was the Texas Baptist Missions

Foundation. I knew most of them. It was a fantastic experience. Jim had become a great friend. He was so knowledgeable and had led several tours to Israel. It was a lifetime dream. The men were available all the time to assist me and keep me from falling. My photo with Jim in Israel.

Chapter Eleven

MY FAMILY

I am writing the chapter on my family. I could write several books. I have tons of letters, etc, that I have sent through the years, but there is not time nor space for all of that. I spent today reading through most of it. It was a deeply emotional experience. It is difficult to decide what to leave out. I have helped my family a lot financially but will not include any of that. All have had their share of problems and hard decisions, but my counsel will remain with them. There were times when the preacher in me showed up. Jane and I chose to help all of our family financially. Maybe we helped them too much, but God blessed us so much, we loved sharing it with our family. Through it all, God has redeemed and blessed all of us. Most of the time I was praising them and telling them how much I loved them, and how very proud I am of them. Jane and I had four wonderful children. As of today, I have three children, eight grandchildren and six great grandchildren, and many spouses. Also, because of a second marriage that I will write about later, I have inherited three more beautiful children, seven grandchildren and one great grandchild. A BEAUTIFUL FAMILY.

Next to God, family has always been most important in my life. Jane and I married June 7, 1951. We had a wonderful marriage for almost 60 years, (59 years, 5 months, and 21 days). I will share my life with Jane, our children and their families, the two years that I was single and my marriage to Joyce and her family.

Jane was the most wonderful wife and companion that I could ever have wanted. She shared my Christian commitment. She felt as much called to the ministry as I did. Whenever I felt God's call to move to another church, or even a different ministry field, we prayed about it, felt a real sense of unity in the decision, and Jane began packing for the move.

We had no children the three years we were at the Seminary and I pastored the Graefenburg Baptist Church. We were newlyweds. There was a great group of young adults in the church that worked in the State offices in Frankfort and we had wonderful fellowship with them. After we completed our Seminary degrees, we moved into Louisville, Jane taught school and I completed a second master's degree with Dr. Wayne Oates. We lived in a second floor apartment over Ginny and Elmer Dawson, friends, who grew up in Graefenburg. They were close friends for many years, visiting and traveling with us. Dr. Oates selected six students to work with him as he wrote the book, Religious Factors In Mental Illness. He acknowledged us as contributors to the book. We worked as chaplains in three hospitals and the state mental hospital. We completed all of the training for chaplaincy certification. Dr. Oates wanted me to go into chaplaincy ministry, either hospital or military. I told him I felt called to pastor churches. He said, if you feel that calling, I want to recommend you to the First Baptist Church of St. Joseph, Louisiana. They called me as pastor and after I graduated, we moved there.

We still had no children and Jane and I enjoyed the freedom and joy of just being pastor and wife of a great church. I enjoyed hunting, fishing and free time with the men of the city. Jane did not teach there and enjoyed reading, homemaking, and the ladies of the church. We would travel to Vicksburg, Natchez, Monroe and other places just as tourists and to eat out. After just three years I accepted the call of the First Baptist Church in Umatilla, Florida. Florida was home for us and we were just 40 miles from Ocala where her brother, Scott, lived and 30 miles from DeLand where I went to college and my brother, Walt, lived. We enjoyed time with family. Walt had four young children and they would greet me with, Hi Uncle Bob. I visited so often, they thought it was my name and would say, here comes HI UNCLE BOB. We adopted Cindy while there, March 11, 1956.

I was called as pastor of a large church in Miami. Some deacons and I visited two nights each week. For three years, I baptized every Sunday night. It was a great evangelistic challenge and opportunity. We let a Jewish community use our facilities on Saturdays. Rob was born while we were there, 9/13/58. Jane quickly became mother of two and expecting a third.

I accepted the call of a new church, Hiland Park, Panama City. I led them in a building program. Judy was born soon after we moved there, 9/6/59. We wanted children and the Lord took a while but then gave us three babies in four years. This was a good church but not so demanding and we were able to enjoy our babies. A family in the church with children the same ages became close friends. We spent lots of Saturdays on the lake with them. I bought a boat and all of the adults enjoyed water skiing, and the kids enjoyed swimming and boating. I wrote an article in a mailout weekly. One week I wrote about all of the excuses people use for missing church and applied it to myself in first person. Mom was on our mailing list. She did not recognize the irony and wrote me that she was afraid that when we bought the boat it would affect my ministry. It took me a while to regain her support. We had a good ministry there and it is a big megachurch today.

The Executive Secretary of the Florida Baptist Convention knew of my ministry for starting new churches. He called and asked if I would consider starting a brand new church in Orlando. He said that Disney and secularization was taking over central Florida and we need to start more churches. They bought a home in a new subdivision and we moved in and began services in our living room. It was a challenge, starting a church from scratch. My ministry at first was visiting house to house and getting involved in the community. Talk about an evangelistic opportunity.

We built buildings as we grew with aid from the State Baptist Convention and support of the First Baptist Church in Orlando. In three years we were having an attendance of five hundred. It was a busy pastorate but I would take a two hour lunch break. Jane would have a picnic lunch prepared and we took those three kids for a boat trip on the many lakes nearby.

Jane was a wonderful wife, mother, and grandmother. I could write a book just talking about her sweet spirit and her commitment to her family. When the children were young, she was a stay at home mom. She never taught school or took a heavy responsibility in the church until after our return home from Argentina. She especially enjoyed Argentina. We had a full time maid and Jane was able to devote all her energies to caring for our four babies. We were all adapting to a new culture and lifestyle. The kids had school in English and in Spanish. One of our neighbors, Tota, was like a grandmother to the kids, especially Mary who was one year old. One family in the English church I pastored had children the age of ours and became like extended family. Our kids made friends with our Spanish neighbors and that helped them with the language.

Coming home on furlough was more of an adjustment for our children than going to Argentina. They were older and at first they did not feel that they fit in. They faced what all children face, finding their identity in school, but even harder. We tried to get them to jump right in to scouts, little league sports, and other activities, but they were hesitant. I was working on my PhD and Jane was teaching school, and we were not as available as we had been in Argentina. They worked hard and adjusted well.

Moving to Lubbock was an adjustment for all of us. I had to give full time to teaching and working on meeting the requirements for tenure. Jane did not get a teaching job right away and that was good. Mary was eight years old when Jane began teaching and came home from school to an empty house. I adjusted my schedule so I could be home when she got home. She had a group of friends to play with. I had about six copies of a book I used in counseling titled, Sex Without Fear. Mary thought those pretty red books, all alike, would be great for playing school with her friends. Our next door neighbor, Myra Timmons, taught in the same college that I did. She asked me one day, what is that sex class you have started in our community. She was joking but it was a topic for conversation.

I served as interim pastor and moved my counseling practice to three churches in Lubbock. The family moved with me. Rob found his place in the youth group and especially in a special singing group at Calvary Baptist Church. It was his church until he married and moved from Lubbock. Judy found her place in the youth group at Second Baptist Church and it was her church until she left Lubbock. When Hank Scott asked me to move my counseling practice to Bacon Heights Baptist Church and Jane and I became leaders of the single adult ministry, Mary became very active in the youth ministry. Later, Mary wanted to move to a more active ministry at First Baptist Church and that was her church until she met ministry in the college ministry and they married. That was our church until I retired and we moved to Sun City, Georgetown, Texas. I could write books on our kids, their families and work and how we visited them, and spoiled the grandchildren, but they will have to tell their own stories.

TRAVEL

Boy did we travel. Jane was a public school teacher. We both
had all of the school vacations and summers off, so lots of time
for travel. While the children were home, all of our travel was for
them. We had an airstream trailer and a ski boat. We used two cars
and pulled both of them frequently to a lake about 40 miles from
Lubbock. There were no trees so the trailer was really nice for rest
stops and snacks. All of us enjoyed skiing, including Jane. We
made numerous ski trips to lake LBJ in Austin and rented a cabin
for better skiing. We took a few long distance vacation trips with
the trailer. We had a time share in Ruidoso, N Mex. and spent two
weeks every Summer and Winter enjoying the mountains.

After the kids left home, Jane and I travelled all over the world.
We had eight weeks of timeshare and we used all of them plus extra
trips every year. We were members of RCI, a travel organization
that would exchange our timeshare weeks for resorts any place in
the world. One Summer they gave us four weeks in Europe for
two of our weeks. We had a week in Italy, a week in France, a
week in Spain, and a week in the Canary Islands. We had a train
pass to travel all over from each of those resorts. We loved traveling all over Europe, England, Scotland, Australia, New Zealand,
Thailand, and other places for two week vacations. We also took
two or more week vacations to Florida, Virginia, Vermont, Big
Bend West Texas, Arkansas, Missouri and other places. As we got
older, we really enjoyed 18 cruises. We cruised the North Baltic
Sea with stops at all of the capitals, several cruises around Spain,
Italy, the Greek islands, Alaska, and many cruises in the Caribbean.
In later years it was easy cruising from Galveston.

A travel agent in Ft. Worth became a friend and issued me a
IATA Travel Agent card. Another travel group wanted me to work
with them and gave me a free 18 day trip to Europe. I got placed
with a bus load of Lutheran pastors who knew all of Martin Luther's

experiences, what he did where, as we travelled thru Germany. I heard more than I ever wanted to know. I took two groups to Hawaii and a group of eighteen couples to Alaska.

We traveled to visit our parents every year until their deaths. Jane and Betty were the youngest in their family and very close. Our children were about the same ages. When they were young, we traveled every Thanksgiving from Lubbock to Houston to spend the holidays with them. When I was pastor in Panama City, Florida, we took our ski boat through the inland waterway with our three babies to visit Betty's family in Niceville, Fla. Much of the trip was across a large lake. We did not know that there were small boat warnings. It was a rough, treacherous trip. We took a lot of chances but never had a tragedy. We had our briefcase stolen in the train station in Italy. We were about to board the train with an overnight sleeping compartment to Spain. We had to get a new passport and airline tickets, etc. it was a miracle that we were able to do all of that in one day and continued our trip.

We planned a trip, spending one week in Washington, DC, one week in New York, and a week in the Poconos in Pennsylvania. It was a fabulous trip. We left our car in the hotel garage in New York and used public transportation. As we were leaving for the trip to Pa. we decided to take photos of all the places we had visited. We parked briefly in front of the Merrill Lynch building and it was stolen, with our luggage, the police said, no chance of finding it. The hotel let us stay the night. I got insurance money, we bought necessities, and with a plastic bag in hand, we took a bus to the Poconos, a small town. The bus station there was in a drug store. We had reservations in a fabulous hotel. I had the phone number for the RCI representative in the hotel. I asked to use their phone. She said no one there will come and get you, they don't do that. I called and they said they would pick me up in fifteen minutes. The lady was astonished and asked, who are you. People were so accommodating all week, taking us places, etc. we got a flight home and a new car from insurance. There is no question but that God takes care of us.

There is no perfect place to speak of Jane's passing, but I must share this with you. She left this earth just like she lived her life, completely trusting in God and His perfect will for her. She was active and going as long as she had breath, even when she struggled to breathe. We took a trip to East Texas and she discovered on that trip that she did not have long to live. When we returned home the doctor told her so and he prescribed hospice care for her. We had our family with us for Thanksgiving just two days before her passing. She was jovial and talkative with the family and ate a good meal. She shared this testimony at the table and one of the family captured it on video.

> *I was diagnosed with pulmonary fibrosis back 6 or 7 years ago. The doctor said it's a mild case. I could go along without breathing and it was no problem. Then it began to take a turn for the worse. Then I began to dread those tests. Then, in July, we went to east Texas just to get away for a few days and boy it really hit me. I couldn't breathe. I couldn't go anywhere. I couldn't get my breath. It just really hit me. Well, I thought maybe it was because the wind was blowing so there in the trees. We came back and found out that wasn't it. We went to the doctor and found out that it had really taken a turn for the worse. And so, from then on, we just decided that we were going to live at home, let nature take it as it comes. We will just live. We've had a wonderful life. We have travelled and travelled and travelled, and enjoyed all our travels. But I have never slowed down enough to thank the Lord for anything. You*

know? Well, this has just been a bang up time for me! I've been quiet, I've been still, and I feel his presence. And I know he brought this on me for a purpose, to make me still, to stop, and to stop and count my blessings. So don't ya'll ever feel bad for what I'm going through. I rejoice. I really and truly rejoice! The Lord's with me, He brought it. I can rejoice! I've got the best companion in the world right here, the best children in the world who are ready to help with anything they can. I don't want ya'll to grieve. I want you to be happy with us. Just be happy is all we ask. Because I wake up every morning looking forward to the day. Just to wake up, get my coffee, read, meditate. That's our day. So, I'm not worried about anything. I'm happy. I'm happy and I'm content.

Rob and Judy were with us the night Jane passed. It was a wonderful time together. Rob asked Jane in his usual sweet way, "Am I still your best boy?" Judy slept with Jane that night. We had a very natural, brief conversation. She did not suffer but later slipped on into heaven.

Jane's Memorial service was a beautiful worship experience at the First Baptist Church in Georgetown, Texas.

Jane Pinder
Obituary

Cynthia Jane Hagood Pinder passed peacefully and confidently into the presence of the Lord on November 28, 2010 at the age of 83 after a courageous seven-year battle with pulmonary fibrosis. Jane was a 13 year resident of Sun City in Georgetown, Texas.

Jane was one of seven children born to Reverend Herrin Hampton Hagood and Flora Estelle Duke Hagood of Crestview, Florida. She was preceded in death by her parents and her siblings Nell Hagood of Enterprise, Alabama; Herrin Hagood of Charleston, South Carolina; and Scott Hagood of Ocala, Florida. She is survived by her siblings Thomas Hagood of Conroe, Texas; Ann Weatherly of Columbia, South Carolina; and Betty Gamel of Conroe, Texas.

Jane graduated from Crestview High School. She earned an Associates Degree from Mars Hill College, a Bachelor of Arts degree from Furman and a Master of Religious Education degree from Southern Baptist Seminary in Louisville, Kentucky. She taught elementary school for 20 years.

Jane leaves behind her husband of almost 60 years Reverend Dr. Robert H. (Bob) Pinder. During their life together, Jane served as a pastor's wife, missionary, mother, and schoolteacher. Jane and her husband served in numerous churches and were Southern Baptist missionaries in Argentina for seven years. She was an active member of First Baptist Church of Georgetown, Texas.

Jane is survived by her children Cynthia Howe (Justin) of Kerville, Texas; Rob Pinder (Debbie) of Keller, Texas; Judy Cox (Trent) of Sugar Land, Texas; and Mary Brinkley (Kevin) of Memphis, Tennessee. Jane was also known as "Meemaw" to her eight grandchildren Rachel Watson, Hunter Cox, Jesica Isbell, Lauren Cox, Jared Pinder, Kate Brinkley, Carter Brinkley and Molly Brinkley. Jane also had two great grandchildren, Quentin Padilla and Charlie Padilla.

A memorial service will be held at First Baptist Church of Georgetown, Saturday December 4th at 11:00 AM. Visitation is Friday December 3rd from 6:00 PM to 8:00 PM at Ramsey Funeral Home in Georgetown. Memorials may be sent to the Building Fund at First Baptist Church of Georgetown, 1333 West University Avenue, Georgetown, TX 78628.

MY FAMILY PICTURE, THANKSGIVING 2017

Chapter Twelve

CHRISTIAN STEWARDSHIP

I preached and I practiced Christian Stewardship, not just to support the church and it's ministries, but as a Biblical conviction and lifestyle that every Christian should live. It is to acknowledge that God is the creator and the owner of everything, our lives and all that we possess. He allows us to be stewards or caretakers of some of His great wealth for a short time. The Bible says, the tithe is the Lord's. You can't out give the Lord. I began tithing at age nine when I sold Liberty magazines from house to house. I made a few pennies on each magazine and bought my first bicycle with the coupons they gave me. Later I sold newspapers on a street corner until they allowed me to have a paper route. I worked for McCroy store, and folded Sunday papers all night Saturday night at the Miami Herald. My last years at home, I worked for Vultee Aircraft Corporation on the tail assembly for P38 airplanes.

At college, I had a scholarship, three part time jobs, and pastored a church to pay my way completely through school. When Jane and I married, we made the same commitment, though it was very difficult at times. They did not pay preachers back then like they do today. We could only afford meat once in a while, but we never were in debt, no credit cards. If we didn't have the green bucks, we didn't buy it. We even saved up monthly car payments and bought a new car every four to six years. My older brother,

Bill, used to say, Bob doesn't buy car tires, he just buys a new car. We lived that lifestyle for 60 years of marriage with four children. Not only were we faithful titters, at retirement we started giving a double tithe.

We also gave extra gifts. November 25, 2003, we gave to the Baptist Foundation of Texas, $87,207.81 to establish the Qualified Charitable Gift Annuity, and $87,207.81 to establish the Advise and Consult Fund, both of which to provide money for mission causes. What a joy to receive quarterly reports to see what these funds are accomplishing in God's Kingdom today. For years they were designated to the ministry of Dr. Lee Baggett and his wife Ruthie in Mexico. We visited them in Mexico and have continued to receive reports of their ministry, great friends. In the future these funds will provide an endowment to maintain the ministry of the Dr. Robert H. Pinder BSM Student Building on the campus of Texas Tech University in Lubbock, Texas.

We made a big donation to initiate the building fund for the new Sanctuary for the First Baptist Church in Georgetown, Texas. I served as Co-chair of that campaign.

Jane went with me as long as she was able to the meetings of the Texas Baptist Missions Foundation Board, that I served on for 13 years. At every meeting we would hear thrilling reports from five to eight mission agencies. We wanted to donate to all of them. We gave liberally to buy bicycles for Mexican pastors, to buy Bibles to saturate communities along the Texas/ Mexico border, to build water wells in Mexico, and other causes, but mostly to start new churches and cowboy churches in Texas. For years we have contributed and personally encouraged the ministry of the Texas Baptist Children's home in Round Rock, Texas. The Joy Sunday school class I taught adopted a home of children to minister to.

We were especially generous to our children. We provided a house, rent free, for Cindy and also for Judy, and equivalent funds for Rob and Mary. I have fond memories of Jane going to garage sales and stores to buy clothes for the grandchildren. We cared deeply for our children and grandchildren. It was never considered a cost but a divine investment. It has paid rich dividends. We have a terrific family.

In my estate planning with the help of Keith Gamel, my nephew and personal attorney, and Don Cramer my good friend and estate planner, I have fulfilled a promise I made to the Lord. I told the Lord that I would give half of my estate to my family and half to Missions. I have had a rich ministry in Baptist Student ministry since my college days. I helped to build a new student building at Texas A&M, East Texas and North Texas and pushed for a new building at Texas Tech. When I was informed that the convention was ready to build at Tech but needed a large donation to get the Campaign started, I offered a half million dollars gift to get it started. Bill Arnold, the president of the Texas Baptist Missions Foundation, flew to Georgetown and told me that if I could give more, they would name the building in my honor. I never had that in mind but after much prayer I gave $750,000, and the building will be named the Dr. Robert H. Pinder Student Center. WHAT AN HONOR, REACHING STUDENTS FOR JESUS FOR GENERATIONS TO COME. I have established an endowment, the DR. ROBERT H. PINDER ENDOWMENT for the Baptist Student Ministry at Texas Tech University, to provide continued support for that ministry to students. Jeff Kennon, a former student of mine has been director of that ministry for over ten years. I have established another endowment for the CRU, Campus Crusade for Christ, student ministry at Tech, directed by Trace Hunt, another former student of mine.

FINANCES

I had been a Baptist pastor for 17 years, eight years with the Southern Baptist international mission board, got my PhD in two years with four children. They gave me a job teaching while I was working on my PhD and God called me with a new calling. God said Bob the greatest need in the world is the USA and the greatest need in the USA is the family and I became a missionary to marriage and family life. I got a job teaching at Texas Tech. I had to borrow money from three different sources to make a down payment on a small house in Lubbock, Texas. I paid off that debt and used the house as the down payment for what became our permanent home in Lubbock. I was very busy but I loved everything I was doing. My dean, Dr. Longworth, had been a dean in Ohio and moved to Lubbock and transferred ownership of his eighty duplexes. He encouraged me to get started in real estate. When I had saved up a little money I bought my first duplex. Jane thought I had gone stark raving crazy, but she pitched in and helped me. She would make curtains for the windows, even clean toilets, do whatever was necessary and we saved up money and bought a second duplex. I put all that they would allow into my 401(k) because I knew we needed to save for the future. I was a full-time tenured professor at Texas Tech in the human development family studies department. I had more than a full-time counseling practice. I never had a secretary or a paid office. Several churches invited me to use an office in their church for counseling. I would have doctors come to my classes for special speeches and as friends they would recommend people to me for counseling. I preached in almost every Baptist Church in the area and built up a clientele of people who would come and send others to me for counseling. First Baptist Church Amarillo really used my services. They had a beautiful home in the Baptist encampment in Glorietta, New Mexico and I had several marriage enrichment retreats with that church. Young couples we're having lots of trouble in their marriages and I would sit in the back of the bus and counsel one couple after another both coming and returning from those retreats. The head of the young married couples department at First Baptist Church Amarillo was the president of the bank. He said Bob we have a branch of our bank on Bell Street and a part of that building we are not using. Would you consider coming on Saturday and we would line up couples for you to counsel. I went every Saturday for more than a year. His wife would have twelve to fourteen couples lined up for counseling.

I also did workshops, speaking engagements, marriage enrichment retreats, and family life conferences all over the USA. One year I was gone forty-two weekends. They were like revivals. God really blessed and used those family life conferences. I will never forget a weekend conference that I had in Spartanburg, South Carolina. I did not know the pastor, but the educational director and I were in college together. He had heard about my ministry and invited me. The pastor had never heard of family life conferences and he told me later that he started to go fishing that weekend and thought that the educational director could handle things. That was one of the greatest weekends I have ever experienced. I would begin those conferences on Friday night just going over some family issues. Saturday morning we would have a breakfast for men only. I really had a strong ministry with men. I felt that they were the key to family life and if they ever got turned on it could really change a family forever. This church was used to having men at a breakfast and we had 700 men to show up for breakfast that Saturday. Their hearts and lives were really touched as I encouraged them to take the lead in their family life. They went home and told their wives and the women turned out in large numbers. On Saturday night I had a mini marriage enrichment retreat and marriages were touched. Sunday morning we had a service including the Sunday school hour and the worship hour and I preached on the theme, God really does care about family life. Oh how God used that message. When the invitation was given over half the congregation were down at the altar, committing their lives and marriages and families to the Lord. The pastor wrote to me later and he said we have all the great evangelists to come to our church. We've had some great revivals but he said God used that family life weekend to bring the greatest revival our church has ever experienced. I had similar experiences in small churches and other large churches.

God used me to speak at special conferences that the Baptist had at Glorietta, New Mexico, and Ridgecrest, North Carolina. From college I knew Louis Wilkerson who headed up the family life magazine at the Baptist publishing board. He and others from the family life department had me come to Nashville for a week-long meeting with their whole staff to bring them up to date on what is happening in family life today. I will never forget preaching and leading conferences at the singles conference one year with over 3000 single adults at Glorietta, New Mexico. I preached in the closing service. The song leader lead the group in singing," Something beautiful, something good, all my confusion God understood. All I had to offer him was brokenness and strife but God made something beautiful out of my life." There was not a dry eye in the auditorium. What a closing session we had for that week.

My SECOND MARRIAGE AND FAMILY

After Jane's death, memorial service, and everybody went home, I was devastated. I stayed busy but I was lonely. I would alternate between trying to stay busy and keep my mind on other things, and focusing on Jane. I would get out the album on our 50th wedding anniversary and other photos, and spend time on precious memories. I signed up for the grief class in our church. I knew a lot about grief, as a pastor, Bible teacher, counselor, and I led grief support groups. However, I knew that when it happens to you, you have to work through it. It takes a plan and a lot of time. They wanted me to teach the class. I said, no, I am here as a patient. It was a great program. The leaders were fantastic. It was interrupted by a planned trip to Israel.

I read a daily devotional by Dr. James Denison. He had a Bible tour of Israel planned. I signed up for it and later discovered that I knew most of the people going. There was a large group from the FBC, Lubbock that I knew, including three families I had counseled. It was sponsored by Texas Baptist Missions Foundation Board that I had served on for thirteen years. It was a wonderful experience. Some of the men were always helpful with my balance problems.

After returning from Israel, I signed up for the next grief class. Joyce lost her husband about that same time and was enrolled in the class. Although we both were very active in church, we did not know each other. I was determined to never marry again and had no interest in dating. I had several invitations to the Solo group in Sun City, but never attended. Several of my friends found companions through a Christian dating group, but I had no interest. Joyce and I shared a lot in the grief sessions. We both were ahead of the group in working through our grief. I invited her to join me for a meal and we met at the soup or salad restaurant. We had a great conversation, but left with no further plans. Two months later, she invited me to her home for dinner. She was a new Christian. In all of my ministry, I had never known anyone so hungry to have a good relationship with Jesus. She had lots of questions and I tried to provide some answers. We became prayer partners and studied the Bible together. This is Joyce's version of our relationship and marriage.

JOYCE, OUR MARRIAGE
We met in a grief share class. Bob was talking about a good testimony that his wife gave and it was videoed. She gave it a few days before she died. I told him I would like to see it. He had to show me how to see it. So in a funny way, Jane put us together. After knowing I could do fine without the class I quit going. I think Bob quit about the same time I did. A few weeks *later he called me and invited*

me to lunch. Since I had no interest in dating I didn't want it to look like a date so I insisted I would meet him there and pay my own way. He said ok and we had a nice lunch. I am not sure how long after our lunch I decided to have a singles dinner party. Nothing fancy but I invited my neighbor who had just lost her husband a month before my husband. I also invited a good friend that was also single. I also invited Bob. Bob right away said he would come. He would never pass up a free meal. My neighbor friend was still quite depressed so she turned me down and my other friend had other plans. I thought this wasn't going the way I had planned. Well since Bob was the only one coming and he was eating meals on wheels at his home, I decided to cook a real down home meal. I cooked a pot roast. Little did I know that it was one of his favorite meals. After we ate we talked for quite some time. It was a very nice evening. He learned that evening that I was a new Christian for about seven years. We became good friends and he would come to my home to read the morning devotional together. That was the start of our relationship. It grew with time. I had no intention of ever getting married again but it was getting serious. My daughter tried to talk me out of getting serious and tried to talk me into just having fun and date different men. I told her that I had no interest in dating. However, I guess God had other plans. I am convinced that God never wants either one of us to be lonely. When my children saw how happy I was they felt differently and were very happy for us when we told them we were getting married. However, Bob's children were not happy about it. Bob asked his son if he would be his best man and he refused. I know that had to really hurt Bob's sweet heart. With a little time though, Rob changed his mind and was his best man. My daughter, Debbie, stood up for me. Everyone at our church was so happy about it. One member told us she thought we were made for each other. Over time though, Bob's children were accepting of me. Mary told Rob, that it was better that I was with Bob then to have them have to worry and take care of him. Lauren made a comment to Judy when they were shopping one day at some mall when they saw a man sitting alone on a bench how happy she was that her Popi didn't have to be alone. I think that really grabbed Judy's heart and she has been so happy for us since then. After we visited Mary and Kevin, Mary bent down to say goodbye and told me that they loved me.

One year later.

We started planning our wedding. We kept it simple and only invited immediate family. We got married April 14 2012. We had a fantastic honeymoon on a cruise in the Caribbean. Putting two houses together was quite a job. We both got rid of a lot of stuff.

August of 2012 we drove to our time share in Ruidoso, New Mexico for two weeks. We got home on a Friday and went to church the next day for an all-day event called FIRST SERVE Georgetown to do services for the community. As we were leaving

Sun City, we had a wreck and hit a tree head on. Bob hurt his foot and I broke three ribs and two vertebra. Bob's foot healed pretty fast but my back was slow. I had to wear a back brace for six weeks. After I got to take the brace off, I took physical therapy for two months. Once I was able to start traveling again things went good for us. We took many awesome trips.

IN 2014, JOYCE WROTE A CHRISTMAS LETTER THAT WAS An EXAMPLE OF OUR LIFE BEFORE HER SURGERIES.

We had another very busy year with our travels. In January we went to Puerto Vallarta, Mexico. We love the resort we stay at there. It is so relaxing and fun. That was our third time there. It is all inclusive so we gained weight. You can't even sit by the pool but that someone is coming by offering you a food menu or drinks. We definitely over indulged while there.

In May, we drove to Branson, Missouri but on the way, we stopped in Mississippi to attend Bob's grandsons graduation at college. From there we went to Nashville, Tenn. to visit Bob's niece. We stayed there for a couple days and then drove to Memphis, Tenn. to attend Bob's other granddaughter that graduated high school plus it was her mother's birthday so we took them out to dinner to celebrate both occasions. From there we drove to Branson and had a great time there. Of course we went to Sight and Sound while there. That was fantastic as usual.

Next, we flew to Alaska and took the land tour of Denali National Park and then hopped on a train with the glass dome roof and had a most beautiful trip to the Ship that we took for the cruise home. I took about 300 pictures on that trip. I think it was the most exciting trip I ever took, equal to the honeymoon cruise we took on the Mediterranean Sea, to Spain and Italy.

Next, in Nov. we went back to Branson and met Bob's son and his wife and also Bob's daughter and her husband there. We had a great family time together.

When we left Branson, we drove through Oklahoma and stopped by my granddaughters home to see my first great-grandson for the first time. We didn't stay long because we still had a very long drive home.

Now we are settled down for a little while but in January, we will be driving to Houston to hop on another cruise ship. I will add those events to next year's newsletter at Christmas.

Then my back started acting up again. We still traveled but it it was getting too hard for me to walk or sit because a cyst formed in the vertebra that was broken in the wreck. After many trips to pain management doctors they decided to do surgery. I finally after a year of pain had the surgery on February 12, 2015. Then I had more recuperation from the surgery and had to start physical therapy again. After healing we had a year of normal happy life again.

My tremors were getting worse so decided to go to a Neurologists. I was told there is brain surgery that can really help my tremors. It was so bad that Bob had to sign my name on things that needed my signature. Bob scouted all over the country to find a good brain surgeon. We didn't just want anyone fooling with my brain. He found a doctor that does it in Houston. We made an appointment with him. He called Bob and told him that he had only done five of those surgeries but that there is a surgeon in Austin that has done hundreds. That was a miracle from God for sure. We set up an appointment with him (Dr. Patel). He explained how it was all done. That was pretty scary stuff and if that wasn't scary enough, I looked it up in the internet and saw a movie of how it was done. Since I have a history of years of migraine headaches I decided I couldn't stand the thought of surgery in my brain. I figured I would be having continual migraines for the rest of my life. One evening I told Bob I wasn't going to have the operation. He tried his hardest to talk me into it but with no success. Finally as a last resort, he told me to pray about it. I prayed that night in bed and finally fell asleep. In my dream that night, I heard Jesus say, "GET AWAY FROM HER SATEN, SHE BELONGS TO ME." That morning when I awoke I told Bob I was going to have the operation. We had it scheduled for the first week of January 2016. That was quite an ordeal. My head was totally shaved the day before the first of three surgeries. Bob got to watch the first one. I was awake for the first two surgeries. The surgeries were a success.

TEN MONTHS LATER

We decided to drive to Lubbock Texas to visit family, friends and see a Texas Tech football game. That evening we met friends and family at Buns Over Texas for dinner. We enjoyed seeing everyone and after eating we went to my granddaughter's home for more visiting. They had a cat and since I like to pet cats, I sat on the sofa petting the cat. All of a sudden I felt a horrible pain in my chest. I broke out in a sweat and laid on the floor. They immediately called the ambulance. The EMS took me out in the ambulance and gave me aspirin and Nitroglycerin. That eased the pain pretty fast. I stayed in the hospital three days. They ran all kinds of tests including a stress test. I passed the tests. They decided to do a blood test before releasing me and it was all clear. Since those blood test aren't always correct they decided to do another blood test. That test showed a problem. So they decided to take another blood test and that one came back all clear. So I was released and we went home.

One week later I had a horrible pain in my chest again. I guess God wasn't done with me yet because I should have died that night. Since we thought it was heart burn. I knew it couldn't be heart burn because the pain was unbearable. My daughter drove from Austin to Georgetown to care for me. She is a Registered Nurse. She kept me on the phone until she got to our home. She sat beside me and I looked up to her and said I need to go to the hospital. She drove Bob and me to the hospital.

*When we got there they put me in an ambulance
and rushed me to the heart hospital in Round Rock.
The cardiologist was waiting for me and they took
me right into the operating room. I had Dissection
of my Coronary Artery. The doctor had to use two
stents to repair the tear. The lining of the artery
had blocked it 100%. I never had high blood pres-
sure or any problem with high cholesterol but now
because of that heart attack, I have heart disease.
I was told that 80% of the people that have these
die right away. I prayed just before they put me to
sleep and told Jesus that I was anxious to see his
face but not yet because I still have some things I
need to take care of first. He answered my prayer
and saved me. I was a fraction of a minute near
death. Again, I had a long recovery period.*

Joyce has three children, seven grandchildren, and one great
grandchild. We live close to Linda and her family and that has been
a special treat, especially since Joyce's health has caused us to limit
our travels. Linda wrote this very sweet letter for my book.

My Adopted Father Bob!
*Bob and my mother met at church and began
dating. I had never seen my mother so happy and
was thrilled to find out more about Bob and what a
wonderful person, husband and father he was! He
is a very outgoing, friendly, and loving person and
you can sense that about him very quickly. Soon
after they married, I entered the most difficult and
dark days of my life. I was going through a divorce
after 32 years of marriage, and shortly after sep-
arating was diagnosed with breast cancer. It was*

155

very overwhelming, and incredibly scary. I had to endure chemotherapy, surgery and radiation, all while going through a divorce and going to work full time.

My mother and Bob were truly a God send to me during those times, and still are! I remember driving to their home on a few occasions, truly a mess and on the border of a breakdown, in tears. They were such a comfort to me and I cannot imagine having gone through that without them! Bob treated me like a daughter and was always willing to listen and offer support and encouragement. I always left their home feeling much better, like I could make it through this horrendous ordeal because I knew how much they loved me and had my back. I could truly open up to them about all I was going through, and I never felt judged, just loved. Bob always had great advice for me and helped me to remain hopeful and encouraged during the storm. He always lifted me up and told me how strong I was and how I was going to get through this. They both prayed for me regularly, and I know that got me through as well.

While I was going through all this, my Mom was also having some very serious health issues and was becoming very discouraged with chronic pain, back surgery, brain surgery and a heart attack all within a short time frame. Bob was there for both of us in a huge way! He was our rock! I'm sure that our turmoil's were quite overwhelming for him as well, but he never wavered in his love and support. He was our Jesus in skin, much needed calm, comfort, and support. He always took the time to listen and be supportive.

Fortunately, I have come through that very difficult time. I am cancer free, and enjoying becoming established as a happy, single Mom and hopeful about my future. Bob and my Mom are to thank tremendously for supporting me mentally, emotionally, physically, and spiritually during that time. To say that Bob is "like a Father" to me would be such an understatement, and I now feel he truly is my Father in every sense of the word! Thank you, Bob, for taking me under your wing as a daughter! Your compassion and love for others is inspirational!

Love,
Your old, new daughter Linda ☺

Every Sunday, while I was single, I ate at the Cotton Patch restaurant with a group from our Sunday school class. I ate meals on wheels food all week and I ate the same small steak every Sunday. They asked me how I wanted it cooked and I said, half way between medium and medium rare. One Sunday the waitress returned from the kitchen and asked me my name. I said, Bob. She said from now on just say you want your steak the way Bob likes it. That always worked and some of my friends tried it and said it worked for them, too.

Joyce and I have a great marriage. We have the blessings of both of our families. We travelled a lot. We had a fabulous cruise around Spain and Italy, a great land and cruise to Alaska, several Caribbean cruises, two great weeks to Costa Rica, and regular trips to our time shares at Ruidoso, New Mexico, Arkansas, and Branson,

Missouri. Joyce has had some terrible health problems that I will let her describe to you. She is a strong fighter and is trying so hard to do all that the doctors prescribe for her treatment. Because of her health we have moved into an apartment at Providence Crossings Retirement home in Round Rock, Texas. We love it here. They prepare a special meal for her every meal. There is a wonderful group of Christian residents here and the fellowship is great.

My children planned a wonderful 90th birthday celebration for me. They showed photos and videos of my life and encouraged me to write my life story. Since that celebration I have concentrated on writing my biography, and have withdrawn from most of the activities we have here. Joyce fills her day with all of the planned activities here in our home. She especially enjoys the different exercise and yoga classes every morning.

OUR TRAVELS, JOYCE AND BOB

I told of how Jane and I travelled all over the world our whole marriage. When Joyce and I married, we continued the Bob Pinder tradition of travel. She and her late husband, Ed, had a trailer and spent a lot of time at Ruidoso, New Mexico. So, I bought two weeks of a two bedroom resort where my family had gone for many years. Joyce and I made many trips there. We would stop in Lubbock on the way and spend the night with Glenna Lane, my friend of many years. I taught a large Sunday school class at FBC Lubbock for many years and every time we passed through, about twenty-five of that group would meet us at Buns Over Texas, a restaurant, for an evening of fellowship. We visited often with Walter and Blanche Strickland, good friends of mine who had been members of a class I taught. He had a time share at Branson, Missouri and said he could not travel anymore and they gave us the time share. We travelled there twice a year, Winter and Summer until this year. We bought a time share in Arkansas nearby to enlarge our trips there. With regular trips to those three places, we still planned other special exotic travels.

Joyce had not seen her family in Pennsylvania for many years. I said you need to visit your family, so we planned an extensive trip to Pennsylvania. Joyce will tell about that trip and the Christmas newsletter she sent to her family in 2014.

> *Our trip to Pennsylvania .... We drove to Lancaster, Pennsylvania which I was very excited about because that is where I was born. Since I am the youngest of all my cousins, it was essential for me to visit before they have all passed away. We stayed with Rosie and Fred Joost. Rosie is my cousin and the closest In age to me. I grew up in farm country which was mostly Amish and Mennonites. It brought back a lot of memories. We went to a dairy farm that belonged to my aunt and uncle and when they passed It was handed down to my cousin and now belongs to one of their children. We saw the beautiful farm home my father grew up in. When I was a child, I got to visit and stay for a week at the farm that my uncle owned at the time and sleep in my father's bedroom. My cousins arranged to have a family reunion while we were there. It was In New Holland, Pennsylvania which was only five miles from where I lived. I was so happy my relatives got to meet Bob. We toured an Amish farm that was right beside a Target . Things have really changed a lot since I lived there. There was a section in the parking lot for the Amish to tie up their horse and buggy.*

WOW ! ! WHAT A LIFE, WHAT AN ADVENTURE, TRULY A LIFE WORTH LIVING, A LIFE BLESSED BY GOD. It was a positive, happy, fruitful life of service filled with great joy. If I had tried, I could not have planned my life any better, from early on or at any point along the way. God had planned all the details before I was born. The only way I can even understand it, is to look back over these 90 plus years in gratitude and praise. The only way I can explain it, is by this hymn that I sing almost every morning.

All the way my Savior leads me
What have I to ask beside?
Can I doubt His faithful mercies?
Who through life has been my guide
Heavenly peace, divinest comfort
Ere by faith in Him to dwell
For I know whate'er fall me
Jesus doeth all things well
All of the way my Savior leads me
And He cheers each winding path I tread
Gives me strength for every trial
And He feeds me with the living bread
And though my weary steps may falter
And my soul a-thirst may be
Gushing from a rock before me
Though a spirit joy I see
And all the way my Savior leads me
Oh, the fullness of His love
Perfect rest in me is promised
In my Father's house above
When my spirit clothed immortal
Wings it's flight through the realms of the day
This my song through endless ages
Jesus led me all the way
Sent from my iPad

I really have no regrets in my life. Certainly not everything was perfect, but I feel good about the totality of my life. I have no ill feelings toward anyone. I have had two loving, caring wives. I had four really great children and at this time, eight wonderful grand-children and six great grandchildren. I have tried to serve the Lord all my life. He knows my weaknesses and my failures, yet He loves me with an everlasting love, and has found a way to use and bless my efforts to be faithful to Him.

All of my adult life was captivated by my desire to be like Jesus. I love all of the Bible but especially the New Testament, the full and complete revelation of God and His will and purpose for us. Some Bibles have the words of Jesus printed in red. I often referred to myself as a RED LETTER CHRISTIAN, I loved the words of Jesus most of all. Jesus was completely God as though he was not human, and was completely man as though he was not God. My daily prayer was, I want to be deeply spiritual but totally human. I think that came through in my preaching, teaching, and counseling, and that is what made it so effective. Melinda Thompson in her testimony said that being in my class changed her whole life and saved her marriage. She was raised in a very legalistic, negative, religious environment. She said, "the way you shared so openly your relationship with Jesus Christ but in such every day, human terms and experiences, I received your candor as a genuineness that had been missing in all of the "Christians" I had ever known."

The devotional we read this morning was what I believe is the secret of my life, Colossians 3:17, "whatever you do in word or in deed, do all in the name of the Lord Jesus, giving thanks to God the father through him." Max Lucado said that when he gave up being the lead pastor to be the teaching pastor, people felt it was a demotion. He said a promotion is not a move up the ladder, but a move toward your call. That philosophy has been the secret of my life. Some have wondered why I have worn so many hats in my life. I never left a job because I had to, it was always because

I felt God was calling me to another challenge. As I look back on my life, I can see more clearly God's design. I enjoyed college, Seminary, every pastorate, the missionary work in Argentina, my twenty-three years teaching at Texas Tech University, counseling, leading marriage Enrichment seminars, and Family Life conferences all over the nation. God has blessed and used my life even in these more than twenty-five years of retirement. My ministry at FBC in Georgetown was described beautifully by all of the pastoral team. We took the tour and free meal at the Oaks Retirement Home when they opened up and they asked me to preach. I had a great ministry there as an unpaid Chaplain, preaching every Sunday to some forty-five residents. I am looking forward to the dedication of the DR. ROBERT H. PINDER STUDENT CENTER at Texas Tech University in August, 2019. In the meantime, I have Bible in hand, ready to preach Jesus at every opportunity.

obtained

9 781545 672945